Walks in South Warwickshire

From Shakespeare Country to the Cotswolds

by
John W Parnham
and
Barry R Wills

Meridian Books

Published 1999 by Meridian Books
Reprinted 2003

ISBN 1-869922-38-7

A catalogue record for this book is available from the British Library

Illustrations by Barry R Wills

To Chris and Anne, with love

Meridian Books
40 Hadzor Road, Oldbury, West Midlands B68 9LA

Printed in Great Britain by Franklyn Publicity Ltd., Macclesfield.

Contents

Publishers' Note

Every care has been taken in the preparation of this book. All the walks have been independently checked and are believed to be correct at the time of publication. However, no guarantee can be given that they contain no errors or omissions and neither the publishers nor the author can accept responsibility for loss, damage, injury or inconvenience resulting from the use of this book.

Please remember that the countryside is continually changing: hedges and fences may be removed or re-sited; footbridges and river banks may suffer from flood damage; landmarks may disappear; footpaths may be re-routed or ploughed over and not reinstated (as the law requires); concessionary paths may be closed. If you do encounter any such problems the publishers would be very pleased to have details. Obstructions to rights of way should always be reported to the appropriate local authority at the following address:

Rights of Way Section
Planning and Transportation Section
Shire Hall
Warwick
CV34 4SX

Introduction

The collection of circular walks described in this small volume represent our favourites within this lovely, varied region.

You may on occasions follow, literally, in the footsteps of Shakespeare, but this area has much more to offer than the Bard and Stratford-upon-Avon. You will explore a variety of scenery and villages that rival the better-known parts of the Cotswolds and have their own characteristics and atmosphere.

The walks will take you along ancient trackways and paths, past standing stones, earthworks, country estates and grand houses. You will discover the distinct wooded hilltops of the Arden countryside, offering wonderful views and hidden valleys. The familiar Cotswold stone will be contrasted with the red-brown hue of the Horndon stone at Edgehill and along the Warwickshire/Oxfordshire border. And with rivers and canals providing infinite variety, each walk will offer its own rewards and, we hope, lasting visual memories and the occasional feeling of surprising remoteness.

As well as vital information regarding licensed premises we have included some local and natural history that we trust will add interest to your walk. We have aimed to make the descriptions of the route as straightforward as possible so that, read in conjunction with the O.S. map, you should not find navigation difficult. The longer walks may be divided into two point-to-point journeys if required and 'escapes' have been added to some routes where appropriate. The book is illustrated with sketches of some of the highlights that you can look forward to *en route*.

Transportation should be reasonably straightforward. Not all of the walks can be reached by public transport but we have given as much information as we can about the availability of trains and buses. Please see the note on page viii about this.

We have prepared what we trust will be eighteen wonderful days out for your enjoyment at anytime of the year. However, some take you through land that may prove awkward when corn is very high.

FINALLY – Some of the walks are reasonably demanding and suitable footwear, waterproofs and rucksacks will make for additional comfort. The weather can change, quite dramatically, throughout the day. REMEMBER – whilst the call of the Dales and Fells may be strong there is beauty and tranquillity close at hand.

MOST OF ALL, ENJOY YOURSELF!

John Parnham

Barry Wills

About the Authors

John W Parnham

John teaches Physical Education and is a Fellow of the Royal Geographical Society. He has climbed in the Himalayas and joined expeditions to the Andes, Norway and East Africa.

Having walked all the National Trails in England and Wales, he believes the visual impact of South Warwickshire described in this book stands comparison with more famous areas of outstanding natural beauty, but remains largely hidden, perhaps even to those who claim to know the area well.

His love of Art prompted the collaboration with Barry Wills to produce an attractive and user-friendly guide that he hopes will, in turn, produce eighteen memorable days out (or perhaps thirty-six if walked in reverse the following year!).

Barry R Wills

Barry has taught Art and Design at secondary level since completing his Fine Art Degree and Art Teachers Certificate in the early seventies.

His teaching career was briefly interrupted after his first year due to his ambition to travel, in this case London to Delhi.

Since those early days he has continued to travel and has walked in countries as diverse as Canada, Nepal, Sri Lanka, Borneo, Crete, Egypt and Thailand to name a few.

Barry has remained an enthusiastic walker, finding the countryside around Stratford-upon-Avon just as impressive as anywhere he has been abroad. This is one of the reasons for co-writing this book so that others can share this enthusiasm,

His further interests include painting, which is hardly surprising, music, hi-fi, astronomy, cycling, watching films and spending time with his family.

Using this book

All the walks are circular, delivering you back to your car or, where possible, to public transport. Where public transport is known to be available, brief details are given in the introductory box to each walk. However, changes are not uncommon so for up-to-date information and for news of new services and of old ones which have been withdrawn you should contact:

British Rail	0345-484950
Centro (West Midlands)	0121-200 2700
Warwickshire Traveline	01926-414140
Oxfordshire Travel Enquiries	01865-810405

The sketch maps accompanying each walk are intended to serve as guidance and not as replacements for the appropriate Ordnance Survey maps. Even though you may not always need to use them OS maps are invaluable if in emergency, bad weather or other reason you wish to cut short or re-route your walk. The appropriate numbers of the Landranger (1:50,000) and Pathfinder (1:25,000, with much greater detail) maps are given in the introduction box at the start of each walk, where you will also find grid references (GR) for the starting points, together with other useful information. Some of the walks are also covered by O.S. 1:25,000 Explorer map 205: as more maps in this excellent new series are published you may find further coverage.

If you are unsure about the grid reference system you will find this explained on the Ordnance Survey Landranger and Explorer maps.

Reference points on the map are shown in the text thus: ❶

Distances mentioned in the text are given in metres (m); however, these can be treated as yards without any significant loss of accuracy.

Symbols shown on the sketch maps should be self-explanatory. Historical sites are indicated by $\mathcal{H}$; attractive viewpoints by 〽 .

It is always wise to carry a compass, a basic first aid kit and some food and drink. Secateurs can sometimes be useful.

Location Map

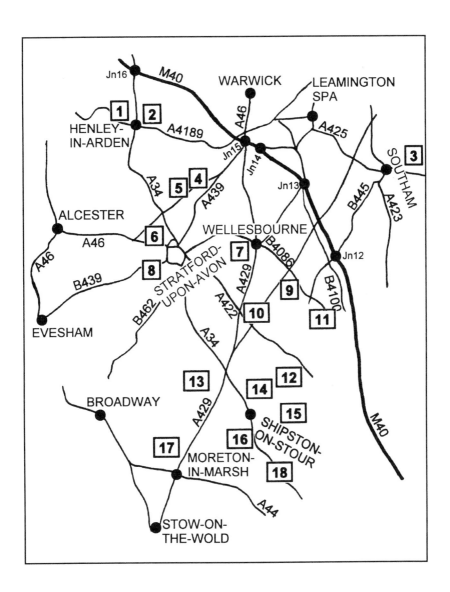

Looking towards Round Hill from the southern edge of Bannam's Wood

1

Henley West and Bannam's Wood

Distance: 11 miles/17.5 km.
Features: Lovely woodland, fine views, ancient tracks.
Terrain: One steep climb. Ridge walking, tracks and paths.
Moderate.
Maps: Landranger 151/150; Pathfinder 998/997.
Car Parking: Beaudesert Lane, Henley-in-Arden.
Public Transport: Trains and Stagecoach bus service X20 to
Henley-in-Arden. If arriving at Henley station cross the railway by
the covered bridge (turning left along the bridge) and start walking
from ★ below.
Refreshments: Pubs in Henley and Wootton Wawen.
Start: Henley-in-Arden. The Parish Church in the middle of the
High Street on the corner of Beaudesert Lane (G.R.152661).

WITH your back to the door of St. John the Baptist, cross over the
road to the newsagents and turn right, passing the White Swan
pub. Immediately take the narrow lane between the buildings
into Shallow Ford Court (Heart of England Way sign).

Carry straight on up through the car park, leaving the pub garden on
your left. Turn left and quickly right to emerge at the end of a cul-de-sac
(Swan Croft). Carry straight on uphill with the Heart of England Way
sign, and drop down the steps to Station Road. Cross over diagonally
left and take the public footpath sign (with handrail) to cross the
railway via the covered bridge.

★ *Rail travellers start here.*

Continue forward along the narrow path alongside the allotments,
take the stile into the field and follow the well-worn path with the
hedge close by on your right. Look ahead and slightly left towards
Bannam's Wood on the horizon. ❶ Our route takes us to this
memorable high point in about an hour. The distinct line of hills to the
left are the Alne Hills including Round Hill which we skirt *en route*.

At the bottom corner of the field ignore the stile that you see straight
on but turn left for 100m to a footbridge under a willow. Cross here and
follow the obvious path and waymarked sign on a narrow ancient track
between the fields, to a stile at the top. Climb the bank and then carry on
in the same general direction as the old track way, across the field with
the hedge on the right for the first 50m only. The chimneys on a cottage
ahead quickly come into view. As you near the cottage, again look
ahead towards the ever closer Bannam's Wood and the delightful
approach that lies in store.

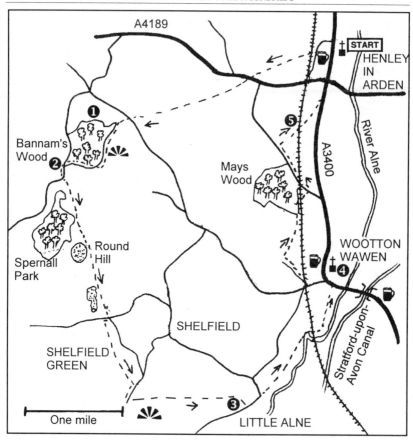

Cross straight over the road, at the black and white 'Well Cottage' and, after 50m or so along the drive, take the stile on the left into the tiny paddock. Leave the paddock quickly and enter a narrow field on the same line. At the far side, take a line diagonally left to the far hedge and waymarked sign. Drop down to the brook via a couple of stiles and a footbridge.

On the far side of the footbridge turn sharp right and pick out a gap in the hedge (with stile) about 150m ahead, a waymarked post in the field helping to guide you. Carry straight on the same line at this stile and another quickly comes into view. Continue straight on at this second stile to a third which is about 100m ahead and is, again, generally on the same line towards Bannam's Wood.

At this third stile cross it and turn right, close to the hedge, to a corner after about 50m. Leave the hedge and take a line downhill and slightly left, to a stile and footbridge at a mid-point in the hedge 200m ahead. Again, this is generally in line with Bannam's Wood ahead. The contours of the hills give something of a wave effect as we begin our ascent, particularly before the harvest and in November as the green shoots of winter wheat appear. (*See O.S. Sheet 150 for onward journey.*)

2

Looking back to Henley from the north side of Bannam's Wood

Cross a stile in the hedge ahead (about 50 yards to the left of the far right corner of the field), then continue on the same line to join the next hedge at a large oak tree and stile. The line up to the top of Bannam's Wood appears obvious and uninterrupted but you do cross an unexpected lane at G.R.123646. Carry straight over on the Heart of England Way, and climb rather steeply to be rewarded with stunning views. Look back to the Parish Church at Henley and above it the mount that is part of the Henley East route. On a clear day you may pick out the two radio masts to the south at Illmington Hill and the Cotswold escarpment to the right. The hilltops are clad with trees which is a distinctive feature of the Arden countryside.

Approaching the wood cross a stile, ignoring another stile and path on the right. Walk with the edge of the wood on your right until the path leads you into the wood through a wicket gate. A sign here (missing when we last did this walk) told you that this is a permissive path and asked you to please close all gates and chains as appropriate, and during the latter half of April, May and June to keep dogs on a lead to avoid disturbing the ground nesting of birds and their chicks.

Follow the obvious route down through the trees on the Heart of England Way – an area that is delightful during bluebell time. At the bottom of the hill, 10m after you emerge from the trees, take the gate on your right. The town of Redditch comes into view ahead at this point. Follow the edge of the field with the hedge on your left. Cross a stile and carry on down to the corner, with an enclosed pond on your right, and take the gate on your left. Carry on for another 100m to a lane to Greenhill Farm. **❷**

Turn left. After 25m, just beyond a right bend, look for two black gates on your left. From the pair of wooden gates take a line straight across the field, equidistant from the fence on the left and the hedge on the right. 50m straight ahead be assured by a waymarker before you descend to a stile in the hedge at the bottom of the field. Cross the stile and footbridge (Heart of England Way).

Ascend the steep and narrow path that becomes enclosed towards the top. Cross the stile to enter a field and carry straight on in the same direction, keeping over to the hedge on the left. Continue to the far left-hand corner of the field to a stile and waymarker. Beyond the stile continue to follow the hedge on the left for 50m until, just before a raised 'dog on lead' sign, the hedge turns sharp left and our route continues straight on across the field, aiming for the gateway at the far left-hand end of the woods ahead.

The track descending from the Alne Hills

Go through the gateway at the left-hand end of the woodland and turn sharp left to arrive at a corner after 100m. Take the gate (H. of E. Way) to the left of the oak tree and then to the stile straight ahead (*not* left), and keep on the same line close to the left-hand hedge. Round Hill comes more clearly into view but, regrettably, our route keeps us to the left. This whole area really is delightful.

Keep to the hedge and eventually a cottage, with two distinctive dormer windows, comes into view. The route emerges on the road via two stiles, just to the left of the cottage, at a pleasant T-junction .

Turn right. After 50m, look for a gate and stile on the left. Leave the road here and take a line straight ahead, with the hedge on your right. Avoid the temptation to drift across to the white cottage on your left. When the hedge bends right continue forward and at the next stile, carry on the same line, this time with the hedge on your left.

Finally, after two fields, emerge on a track. Continue forward for another 200m, on the farm track, to where it joins the road. Turn right.

Follow the road for 400m and, at the houses and post box where it turns sharp right, we turn left at a finger post into a field.

Pause for a moment at the entrance to this field. Our route follows the *left-hand* hedge although there is a public footpath that goes right. Before descending, look straight ahead in the middle distance and, below the line of trees, you can just see the tower of Aston Cantlow

4

Church. Above are the Rough Hills and left is the radio mast at Snitterfield. Follow the edge of the field, ignoring the little footbridge on the left about two-thirds of the way down. You have some all-weather gallops for company on your right

At the corner, take the stile and continue the descent in the same direction, on a particularly attractive track, with the ditch and hedge on your right-hand side. Soon, the rooftops of Little Alne come into view ahead and, at the end of a line of small poplars, join a surfaced track in the same direction. Leave the surfaced track very soon – N.B. Private sign! DO NOT change direction. (*Here return to O.S. sheet151.*)

Continue on the unsurfaced track which after swinging to the right-hand side of the hedge soon reaches a road. You are now on the Monarch's Way, a long distance path running from Worcester to Shoreham on the South Coast, and following the route taken by Charles II after his defeat at the Battle of Worcester.

At the road ❸, turn left and walk past the craft workshops and studios of the Arden Centre on your right.

The hamlet of Little Alne contains buildings of interest on both sides of the road. At the end of the main street, the road swings hard round to the left, towards Wootton Wawen (and is joined by a road from the right). Follow the main road round to the left and, about 50m beyond the bend, take the stile on your right into the field – it is just behind the large directional road sign. Take a line which is at right-angles to the road, close initially to the fence on the left.

Cross the stile in the hedge at the top, and continue diagonally right to another on the brow of the hill. Pause for a moment and have a good look around. Ahead is the impressive church at Wootton Wawen (though this may not be visible in the summer) and, behind, our route from Round Hill is visible (we are actually on another Round Hill – G.R.145616).

Follow the path to the road at Great Mill Farm, turn left and then immediately right, into a field, and take a line diagonally left from here, towards the single red-brick building. Beyond this our route takes us gradually over to the right-hand hedge and our first views of the River Alne. A stile gives access to a lane where we turn right.

After 100m, go under the railway bridge and take the footpath immediately on the left, between the embankment and a concrete surfaced lane. *At the time of writing this path was heavily overgrown and we were forced to cross the cattle-grid and walk along the lane for about 50m. Here we met the stile (on the left) bringing the path onto the lane.*

If you can walk along the path follow this for 50m, then take the stile onto the lane. Turn left on the lane but, immediately begin to leave it, by heading diagonally right to the far right-hand end of the tall fence and stile ahead.

Don't linger here, for reasons that will become obvious, but follow the narrow path between the fence and the river. At the end of the fence, take the stile and keep over to the right. We are still on a general line with the church at Wootton Wawen. Soon going through a hedge gap keep the river on your right and, eventually, after passing a bridge over the river, join a raised embankment as you approach the church, and proceed to the road in a delightful position above old water meadows. ❹

If time allows, the church is well worth a visit and is one of the oldest in Warwickshire. At the road turn left, with the Wootton Wawen Stores immediately on your left. The Bulls Head, a black and white timbered pub, comes quickly into view. Turn left here, onto the Alcester Road, with the pub on your right, and admire Pound Cottage on your left. Continue up this road, alongside the pub car park, until the railway bridge is reached.

Immediately under the bridge, turn right into Gorse Lane. After 450m, the white cottage you pass is Gorse Cottage and, at the end of their garden, look for a right turn to leave the road just beyond a wooden stable block into a field.

Take the stile into the field and then a direct line towards the houses. Take the little concrete footbridge and continue along the same line, with the hedge on your left. At the stile, fork diagonally right for 100m and descend to, and *very carefully* cross, the railway.

Turn right at the stile and proceed, narrowly, between two hedges to emerge at the road. Turn left and cross the road to face the on-coming traffic. Re-cross the railway opposite Mayswood Garage and carry straight on.

Pass The Woodlands cottage, on the brow of the hill, and continue quickly down for 200m until (as a point of reference) the woodland on the left-hand side of the road ends. After another 200m and, before the farm buildings on the left, look for a waymarker post to leave the road on the right. Take a line at right angles to the road, along an old hedge with occasional trees, towards the farm buildings.

Take a stile and continue towards the buildings, to the top of a lane marked by a white gate and, at the time of writing, an abandoned telephone box. Descend to the road, with a school on the right after crossing the railway line. ❺

At the road, turn left. Go straight over the traffic lights and back into Henley High Street. You will soon see the Parish Church. Well done. Reward yourself with an ice cream – rum and raisin to be recommended!

If you have arrived by train now read the first part of this walk for instructions on returning to the station.

2

Shyly Hidden Henley

Distance: 11 miles/17.5 km or 6½ miles/10.5 km.
Features: Fine ridge walking with open aspects and lovely views.
The route follows, in part, the Heart of England Way with ancient,
earthworks, country lanes, woodland and two contrasting
sections.
Terrain: The two climbs and wooded sections can be muddy after
rain.
O.S. maps: Landranger 151; Pathfinder 975.
Public transport: Trains and Stagecoach bus service X20 to
Henley-in-Arden. If arriving at Henley station turn left on leaving
the station and shortly turn right along Swan Croft and follow the
Heart of England Way signs to reach the High Street. Turn right for
a few metres and cross the road to reach Beaudesert Lane.
Car parking: In Beaudesert Lane which is halfway along Henley
High Street, beside St John's Church and opposite the
supermarket and post office.
Refreshments: Pub in Lowsonford.
Start: Beaudesert Lane, Henley-in-Arden (G.R.154660).

WALK along Beaudesert Lane, passing the churches of St John and
St Nicholas and crossing the River Alne. Our route takes us
through the kissing gate at the far end of the lane, and,
following the Heart of England Way, ascends a steep hill known as the
Mount, which is, in fact, a massive earthworks, and marked Motte &
Bailey on the map. This initial shock to the system is quickly rewarded
with spectacular views across the Arden valley to the right. The radio
masts at Ilmington Hill can be seen to the south, whilst Bannam's Wood
is visible on the horizon, above the town. Follow the undulating path in
a delightfully raised position for about 15 mins until it levels out under
some power lines.

Ignore the stile on the right and carry straight on with a waymark
sign. After 250 metres of even going, take a waymark path on the right,
over a stile, and carry on diagonally across the next field to a stile in the
hedge and another waymarker. Cross the stile and turn left and proceed
narrowly, between hedges, for 50 metres then sharp right to emerge
into the fields again.

Carry straight on across the field, heading to the right of a white
cottage. Cross the drive, with a waymark, that serves the white cottage
and descend down the left-hand edge of the field, then forward into a
spinney. Carry on the same line, looking ahead for the waymark sign
and stile. Cross the stile and carry on with the hedge on your right,
staying close to it. After 75 metres bear left to a stand of firs and a gap in

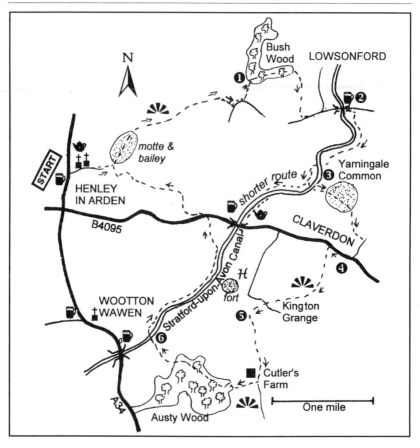

the hedge and another waymark sign. Quickly cross two stiles and descend to the road through two fields, keeping the hedge on your right.

At the road, turn left over the bridge and quickly arrive at a sharp right hand turn where you turn left and proceed up the farm drive to Coppice Corner and Bushwood.

Cross a bridge over a disused railway as the farm buildings come into view but just before reaching them, take the metal gate on the right (still on the Heart of England Way). Keep on the obvious track away from the buildings for about 150 metres and swing round to the left to another metal gate. At this gate, turn right to skirt the edge of the wood. After 50 metres, bear left and very shortly cut into the wood itself at a waymark and enjoy undulating walking through the conifers. However, as leaves on the ground will show, there are many oaks not far from the path. ❶

Carry straight on when emerging from the woods but keeping the trees on your right. After 200 metres turn right at a corner and two stiles and, after a few minutes, reach a lane (having left the Heart of England

8

Split bridge on the Stratford-upon-Avon Canal

Way about 50 metres after the stiles). Turn left and descend into Lowsonford. Straight in front of you, you will soon see one of the white barrel-roofed lock keeper's cottages which are unique to this canal. At the canal our route is over the bridge and right, onto on the towpath. However, if you feel like some refreshment the Fleur de Lys pub is 200 metres on the left before the bridge. ❷

Turn left along the towpath and walk south. Continue for a mile, initially with the canal on the right but changing sides at bridge 44. This is a split bridge – one that allowed the tow-rope to pass through and a cheaper form of construction than the more substantial brick bridges that are more common on other canals.

At lock 34 (Bucket Lock Cottage) we reach another barrel-roofed cottage.

Here the shorter and longer walks separate. To continue along the 11 mile route now continue reading from ★ on page 10.

For the shorter route carry straight on for another mile or so, crossing the canal once more at lock 36. Preston Bagot lock house, built in 1810, is particularly impressive. Note the Stratford-upon-Avon Canal Company sign and the old private fire insurance sign on the wall. Beside it is another barrel roofed cottage. After passing tea-rooms reach the road at bridge 47. Leave the canal here and turn right long the road, passing the impressive Preston Bagot Manor. At the T-junction turn right again and continue uphill, past the Crabmill pub and take the first right at the top of the hill. Now rejoin the main text at ✪ on page 12.

★ Continuing the longer walk cross over to the left-hand side. Do not take the private gate in front of you but, rather, turn left and walk back on yourself on a pleasant grassy bank for 50 metres, or so, and then turn right to descend some steps. ❸

Carry on uphill towards Yarningale Common, first on a path to reach a lane, then follow the lane for about 600 metres to a Give Way sign at an obvious junction (note the post box in the wall on your left). Turn right and then immediately left towards the kennels at Holly Cottage, bearing left just beyond them at a waymark sign to reach a metal gate. Cross the adjacent stile and, with the hedge on your right, carry on to another stile beside a gate about 50 metres ahead. At this stile go straight forward for another 50 m to another stile. Cross this and bear diagonally right across the field, to a mid-point in the opposite hedge to a stile and waymarker. Cross straight over what can be a muddy cross-tracks and straight on up a rutted track with tall hedges on each side.

At the road ❹, and just over to your left, a delightful cedar tree marks the entrance to an imposing house. Pause for a moment at the gate on your left and look back, on a clear day, to a truly magnificent view.

Turn right into the village where a rest may be taken at the seat on the village green opposite the shop, or, at this junction, turn right for 100 metres to the Crown Inn. 100 metres past the pub, leave the main road with a stile and waymarker on your left. Go forward with a hedge on your left, shortly ignoring a path to the left. Cross a stile to join a lane and turn right. Stay on this as it curves round to the left past the Lake House.

Continue on past Breach Manor and a converted barn on your right. Shortly unfolds one of the most spectacular views anywhere in Warwickshire. After 100m pass through a wicket gate, followed by a second in another 100 metres. Note the old farm implements here. You soon enter the woodland over a stile beside a small gate. Go through this narrow piece of woodland for only a few metres. On leaving the trees, keep close to the fence on the left until reaching a stile at a B&B sign (Woodside).

Turn right on the road (not the B&B lane!) and carry on for 75 metres, or so, to where, as the road continues to bear left, our way goes straight on at a stile and waymark sign. Go straight across the field and make slightly left to the corner of the wood to a green gate and old feeding bath. Pause to admire the view before descending diagonally right with a series of waymarked posts, to the road.

Turn right and, after a few minutes, arrive at the hamlet of Kington Grange. Just before a green Dutch barn and opposite Kington Cottage turn left. This lane is signposted Chestnut Rise. ❺ After 250 metres, ignore the farm signs to the right, and take the left fork, leaving the

The hamlet of Kington Grange

buildings on your right. After just a few more minutes walking in a delightful aspect, and after crossing a stile, Cutlers Farm comes into view. Continue forward along the waymarked track for about 800m to reach this.

At the farm leave the commercial offices on your right and, at the end of the buildings, turn right into the main yard (waymark sign). Pass the tennis court on the left and continue forward, soon with a hedge on the left. Walk uphill, steeply at first, until the track swings right and takes you through a gate into the wood. Keep right on the bridleway and keep bearing right following the bridleway signs.

Continue gently downhill, in very pleasant woodland, arriving back at the canal after about half a mile. **6** At the canal, eight miles has been covered. Turn right on the towpath at bridge 51 (another split bridge). Note how the bank falls steeply away on your left, and the obvious engineering problems that would have been encountered.

Cross straight over the lane at bridge 50 and so on for another mile to No. 49. Notice the weight restriction sign and also, over to your right, the wooded hill fort. After another 150 metres, leave the canal at right angles on your left. Cross the footbridge and ascend the obvious path straight across the field. It is worth pausing halfway up to look across to your right to enjoy the view of the isolated church at Preston Bagot on the horizon. Notice, also, how the canal has disappeared behind you.

As you approach the two detached houses, just slightly left join another track and continue on the same line until you reach the road via a gate. Turn right and, at the fork, our route lies to the left. **7** However, if refreshments are required, you can take the right fork and descend for 200 metres to the Crabmill pub).

Having taken the left-hand fork, after only a further 50 metres cross the main road.

✪ *Here the shorter walk rejoins the main walk.*

Follow the lane for a few minutes. At a three-way fork, take the middle route (avoiding the descending track on the right that leads to the impressive farm). After 50 metres, pass a solitary house on the left. Cross the stile ahead, keeping on the same line but slightly left, to a gate in the hedge opposite (north).

Go through the gate, then diagonally left to a mid-point in the hedge to your left and, at a stile (this is only 50 metres), go right and quickly left following the waymark signs. The going is pretty obvious here. Carry straight on, through a number of small paddocks with gates and stiles, and following waymarks to the road. Turn right, but only for 10 metres, and then immediately left at the stile.

Go straight on, with the hedge on the right-hand side, for only 100, metres and, before the corner, turn right through the hedge and go diagonally left for 20 metres, or so, into the woods, descending the steps to the playing field.

Skirt the edge of the playing field to the right, through the gate, and so on through a gap between the houses. Cross straight over the road and follow the path around the school playing field, and then keep left on the made-up path (ignoring the stile ahead that leads into the field). After passing a housing estate we are quickly back at Beaudesert Lane after what, we trust, you have found to be a truly memorable day.

3

Lower Shuckburgh and Napton-on-the-Hill

Distance: 9 miles/14.5 Km or 5 miles/8 Km.
Features: A canal towpath section. Fine views. The impressive
Shuckburgh Estate. The interesting hill village of Napton with its
fine windmill.
Terrain: Moderate. Two climbs.
Maps: Landranger 151; Pathfinder 977.
Car Parking: Roadside in the village.
Public Transport: Nothing suitable.
Refreshments: Pubs in Flecknoe (weekends only) and
Napton-on-the-Hill.
Start: Lower Shuckburgh off the Southam/Daventry
road(G.R.489627)

FACE the church at the war memorial and follow the road to its right (leaving the church on your left). About 200m down here there is a parking place on the right and, just beyond this, is a white railed bridge over the Oxford Canal. Cross the bridge (bridge no.104) and turn right towards the canal towpath. Do not go onto the towpath but join the Oxford Circular Walk (signed here to Rugby) and walk forward along the bridleway with a hedge and the canal on your right. After a few minutes, pause to look back across the meadow to the village church at Lower Shuckburgh, in a delightful location.

Leave the bridleway when you reach the first canal bridge (No. 103) ❶ and turn right across it. 20m beyond the bridge turn left at the waymarker and follow the wide double track across the field. At the far end we are reassured by a waymark post, just slightly hidden, on our left. Our route continues in the same direction, gradually swinging right away from the canal, with Bush Hill becoming more and more prominent on our right.

On the far side of this second field we are re-assured by a waymarker. Continue straight across the third field until we draw level with the wooded hollow on Bush Hill to our right and a waymark post directs us right. Turn right through the gap and follow the edge of the field, climbing steadily, with the hedge on your right. The houses on the outskirts of Flecknoe, with a large cedar tree, come into view straight ahead.

Continue to the corner of the field, turn left for 20m, and then go right, through the gap. Turn right, then left, to carry on in the same direction, uphill and next to the hedge on your right. You are still going in the general direction of the cedar tree. Continue into the corner so

13

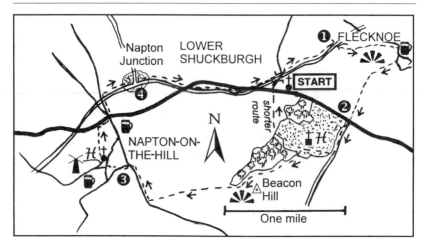

that the cedar tree is 100mto the left. Turn left to the gate and go through it onto the lane just by the old vicarage. Salute the flag as necessary! Pause at the gate and look back at the already impressive views. Don't be tempted off the lane by various waymarkers.

Continue along the lane into the village. At the junction at the end of Vicarage Road, with the old chapel on the right with its twin yews at the gate, turn left into the village if the pub is required but remember it is only open at lunchtime over the weekend (i.e. not weekdays). (You will need to retrace your steps to this point). The old Olive Bush pub is worth a visit but, if the temptation is resisted, turn right at the junction, passing the old chapel on your right and then turn right into Bush Hill Lane (not as far as the telephone box ahead). After 100m the lane swings round to the left. Continue to follow it, ignoring the waymarker post ahead.

At a fork, bear right in front of a cottage with a stone statue of a girl in the garden and a small sycamore tree. Follow the track to the left of the cottage, leaving it on your right. At the top of the lane is a metal sign for Hill Farm bungalow (on a plough blade). Don't go straight on here but keep round to the left for 50m, until you reach a large green farm building with a 'Bates Farm' sign. Turn right, and keep tight over to the hedge on your right. The going, in this section, is indistinct at times and can be awkward when crops are high: however, you will soon be rewarded with fine views.

Continue for about 300m until you reach the corner of the field. Turn left for 10m and go through the gap by the old ash tree (there is a waymarker for travellers in the opposite direction). Turn sharp right and follow the edge of the field as our route swings round to the left and downhill for a further 100m, with a wire fence on the right. From this point, at a junction of fields and gates, look over, diagonally left, to spot a single red barn in the middle distance (our route is just to the left of

14

The church and house, Shuckburgh Park

this), and beyond it a variety of trees including pines in Shuckburgh Park that is *en route*.

From this corner (there are again waymarkers on the right but in the opposite direction), do not go through the gap straight ahead but turn left along the edge of the field, keeping the hedge on your right, in the direction of the estate trees ahead.

We are now walking along the edge of a considerable field. Don't be tempted through the gap half way along, but continue in the same direction with the hedge on your right. Keep on until a waymarker re-assures you in the far corner.

Carry on in the same direction across a field, getting closer all the time, to the red brick barn over to your right. Also visible is the private drive and gatehouse that is the private entrance to the deer park (our route is some way to the left).

With the barn about 150m to the right, carry straight on, at a gap in the hedge, in the same direction. Cross two fields, via a single plank footbridge ❷ and keeping a hedge on your left, to eventually arrive at the road. Turn left on the road for only 10m and then cross straight over and proceed up the tarmac drive with the wooden deer fence on the right.

As you continue, the house itself comes into view on the right, with the church to the left of it. A right-hand turn takes us into the deer park next to a lodge with ornate chimneys. There is a waymarker and we proceed through a tall gate. (This is Back Lodge). Follow the track towards the church with a wall on the left initially and then on past the

15

arch in the stable block. About 50m, beyond the stable block, leave the drive diagonally left and proceed across the grass, (this is before the fork in the track, the right-hand one of which goes to the house).

Leave a sycamore and a dying chestnut to your right, about 100m from the drive, and swing round to the left under the power lines towards the stile at the left-hand corner of the woods. Each time we have walked here we have seen a buzzard and the woods are delightful around Easter with bluebells.

Here the shorter and longer walks separate. To continue on the longer route now continue reading from ★ below.

Taking the shorter route simply continue across the estate, keeping the church on your right, and eventually descend back to the village of Lower Shuckburgh.

★ Continuing the longer walk do not enter the woods but take the stile to the left and carry straight on, leaving the trees to the right but staying close to them. After 200m we are re-assured by a waymarker at a large metal gate and a blasted oak. The way is obvious as we climb along the edge of the woods with some enclosures.

At a junction of tracks ignore a stile on the left and continue to a gate, where the ground levels out. Make diagonally right but maintain height, rather than dropping down to the woods. Aim for the left-hand edge of them. As long as you maintain height and keep the trees about 75m to your right, you will spot the trig point over to the left, on Beacon Hill. It is worth pausing here to take in the view. As you descend to the corner of the woods, take the stile and then turn sharp right to continue to follow the trees. Enjoy some delightful views.

Follow the wide track as the village of Napton-on-the-Hill comes into view, with its windmill, in the middle distance.

Continue right to the bottom of the hill. Beyond where the trees finish there is a barn complex on the left and two stiles close together on the right. Take the stiles and footbridge and turn sharp left on the same line, across the field (with wire fence at time of writing).

On the far side, take the stile (don't feed the horse), turn left on the lane and go through the gate (after only 20m), and then turn immediately right off the lane and follow the edge of the field. (A diagonal path sometimes leads across the field, depending on the time of year that will take you to the same place). Power lines are 50m to our left. However, proceed down the edge of the field to the corner.

Do not take the gap ahead but follow the edge of the field round to the left, with hedge on the right. Cross beneath the power lines. After another 200m, take the stile on the right and footbridge. Continue diagonally left to cut across the corner of the field to a waymark post and waymarker. Cross the stile and take the line diagonally right across the field towards Napton.

Napton Junction

On the far side, continue through a gap, in the same direction, and look for another stile and waymarker straight ahead.. Carry straight on to the road where a large fishing lake comes into view and you turn right. ❸ Follow the road for 200m and then take the first left to Napton (half a mile). After 150m, look for a stile on the right and leave the lane here. Head up, diagonally left, towards the double telegraph poles. Cross the wooden fence and carry on, keeping left, to a waymarker (after 50m) at a stile in the corner.

Cross straight over the lane and keep straight on up the next field in the general line and to the right of the double telegraph poles and carry on up to the houses. Take the stile next to the ivy-covered wall of The Granary and into Vicarage Road. Cross straight over to the left of the cream coloured cottage (with weighing scales), and take the tarmac path alongside its garden (with brick wall) on the left. The steep path levels out at the drive that serves the church to our left. (If you wish, follow this round to the right of the church to the windmill, for a quarter of a mile, and return to this point).

Cross straight over on the old tarmac path, to the kissing gate and continue in the same direction, via a series of gates. Don't worry about not taking refreshment at Napton, another hostelry is *en route* ahead.

Descend, quite steeply, to the main road at a junction. Cross straight over to the post box and 'The Old Barn' and turn right on the pavement. After 200m, on the right is 'Ye Olde Kings Head' which makes a welcome break. Just beyond the pub and in front of the garage, turn left.

Carry straight on, passing a left fork, for 400m to the canal bridge. Cross the bridge and turn right onto the towpath, via a little metal gate. Pass Napton Marina very soon on the opposite side. (Again make sure the water is on your right, otherwise you could end up in N.W.1!).

17

Cross the bridge at Napton junction, ❹ where we are joined by another canal, and continue in the same direction. Where the Oxford Canal joins the Grand Union Canal would have been an important junction in the days of canal transport. You will go under the road bridge (no.108). The village of Lower Shuckburgh comes back into view, as does Bush Hill beyond it. As you draw level with the village, you arrive at bridge 105, which is a footbridge. If you left your car near to bridge 104 you may like to continue along the canal the short distance to it and leave the towpath there. Otherwise leave the towpath immediately before bridge 105 and cross the canal. Take a straight line across the field towards, and just to the right of, the church.

Follow the rusty barbed wire fence for a short distance, as it curves round to the right, and look for a small metal gate and waymarker on your left. Proceed, narrowly at first, and then onto a lane to find yourself back at the war memorial.

4

Snitterfield and Hampton Lucy

Distance: 11½ miles/18.5 km or 8 miles/13 km.
Features: Some fine views, an impressive monument, an interesting riverside section and an impressive village church.
Terrain: Undulating. Moderate.
Maps: Landranger 151; Pathfinder 998/997; Explorer 205.
Car Parking: In the village square.
Public Transport: Stratford Blue service 24 from Stratford-upon-Avon. Alight at the Foxhunter Inn.
Refreshments: Pub in Hampton Lucy.
Start: Snitterfield G.R.213598.

START with your back to the front door of the Foxhunter Inn in Snitterfield, which is in the village square, and proceed straight up The Green, with the Methodist Church on your right.

The road takes you out of the village through a conservation area, with a number of individual cottages. Follow this passing the large cedar tree on your right in the garden of The Wolds. After half a mile you arrive at a T-junction at Gospel Oak Lane. ❶ Leave the road here by taking the stile with waymarker straight ahead. After 50m, take another stile with the fence close by on the right. After a further 100m, cross the little footbridge, and turn immediately right around the edge of the field.

This following paragraphs may seem like overkill but there is massive potential for frustration and navigational disaster! Beware!

The field is long and narrow and swings round to the right. Follow the right hand edge, until its width is reduced to only 20m. At this point there is a waymark post which takes you diagonally across the field to the end of the left-hand hedge (about 100m ahead).

Stand with your back to the long field, with the hedge end just on your left. Immediately left you will see a radio mast as a point of reference and, to your right, look across the entrance to the narrow field to a gap in the hedge. From this point take a line diagonally left (SW) across the large field in front of you. This may not be clearly marked at certain times of the year. Very quickly a hedge comes into view on the far side of the field and it becomes obvious that some of the trees, apparently on the far side, actually form a wooded hollow within the field rather than on its far edge. Our line skirts the left-hand edge of this hollow.

19

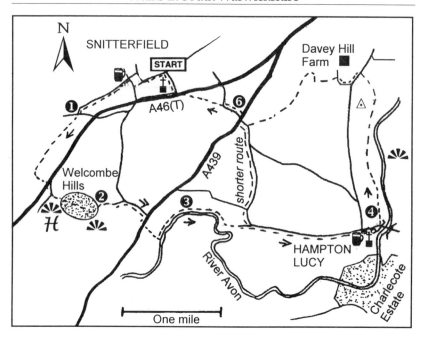

If you have taken the precise line across the field you will arrive at a waymark post. In any case turn sharp left at the edge of the field and follow it with the hedge on your right

You will now get your first view of a major landmark, and one that remains with us for most of the day. This is the large monument on the Welcombe Hills marked as obelisk on the O.S. map ❷, and is our next point of interest *en route*.

Follow the edge of the field and descend a short tarmac drive. Cross the road *with care* and proceed through the gap onto the old Stratford Road and turn right. After about 100m the road passes between houses but, before dropping down sharply right, leave the road at the brow of the hill where it is signposted by Round House Farm and carry straight on towards the monument. Proceed straight on through the first gate as the path narrows, with some delightful views over Stratford to your right. After passing through a narrow strip of woodland arrive at a second gate (with two old cogs for counterbalance).

Our route is immediately left again, through another gate, but it is worth pausing and wandering 20m right to a bench to enjoy the views. However, turn left through the gate and proceed, for 150m, on a well-worn path with a wooded area, containing some tall Scots Pines, on your right to reach another gate. Proceed through this and turn immediately right through another where the path is obvious towards the monument, with the roof and chimneys of the Welcombe Hotel coming into view on your right with its walled garden. By contrast, the horizontal concrete lines of the NFU building are visible straight ahead across the valley.

Take a diagonal line across to the monument to read the inscription at its base:

'A good, wise and brave man. A friend of liberty in evil days.' This was erected in honour of Sir Hugh Clopton, a wealthy merchant who was born in Stratford and became Lord Mayor of London in 1492. He was a generous benefactor to the town and built the fine bridge across the Avon in Stratford.

Afterwards, cut back left to rejoin the original path near an isolated cottage and proceed downhill, through a gate and on down a long straight drive to the road, passing a golf course on your left. Where the drive meets the road there is a Welcombe Hills information board that is worth a look. Turn right and follow the road downhill to the main

The Clopton obelisk

Stratford-Warwick road where you turn right and follow the pavement for 100m. On the opposite side, a group of poplars mark the entrance to a new building. Just beyond this, cross the road and take the track, with waymark post, and marked by two grindstones (one with its mechanism intact). The ground has now levelled out as we approach the river. Follow the track as it turns left and then right with barns and an ancient green caravan on the left, as a point of reference. 100m further on note a line of small willows joining from the right and, as you draw level with these, look for a sign and stile on the left to take us into a field towards Hatton Rock and Hampton Lucy.

Stay close to the fence on your right and pass the old bath water trough into the corner where you turn left, to find yourself suddenly close to the River Avon (though it may not be visible in summer). Immediately go round the small mound to its left but generally stay close to the fence on your right.

We are now approaching a delightful, quiet, riverside section, with a remote feel and rather unique atmosphere. Unlike the more familiar stretches of the Avon below Stratford it is not navigable. There are some interesting species of plants here.

When you reach the old wind pump, take the stile to the right on a straight line below the escarpment on your left. ❸ The area is seldom walked although it is marked as a public footpath on the O.S. map and perseverance through the undergrowth may be required at the height of summer. After 100m, look up left to the stone balustrade and large pine tree as points of reference. Stay close to the base of the escarpment and, after 300m, cross a tributary to the Avon via a footbridge. Turn sharp right to climb steeply up the edge of a field to a delightful raised position, with good views across the river.

Ahead and slightly right is a distinctive church tower at Hampton Lucy, which is our next stop *en route*. Carry on along the edge of the field and descend to another footbridge. Immediately over the bridge ignore a path to the left and pass below a brick-surmounted mound. As you climb away from the bridge, look right to the island and weir near the village of Alveston (there is no way across the river).

As three red brick dwellings appear over to our left, the river swings sharp right and our way is still fairly obvious along the edge of the field. Do not descend until you have gone beyond this bend in the river.

Looking down to the River Avon from the elevated river bank

22

Follow the edge of the field for about 100m and about 15m before the edge swings left and then right look out for an easily missed path descending to the right. Follow this path, with a barbed wire fence on the right. On reaching a track on level ground, turn left and proceed to the road.

To continue the longer walk now continue reading from ★ below.

If you are following the shorter route turn where the path meets the road, then take the first right until you reach the main road. Here rejoin the main walk at ✪ on page 25.

★ Turn right and proceed along the road into the village of Hampton Lucy. The church tower and ornate masonry are very impressive – monument to the wealth and power of the Lucy family.

Charlecote Park, the home of the Lucy family for over 700 years and now owned by the National Trust, is just beyond the village and is certainly worth investigating on some other occasion. William Shakespeare was supposed to have poached deer in its grounds and to have been brought before Sir Thomas Lucy who imposed penalties on him. This interesting story had doubt cast upon it when it was realised that the park did not exist in Shakespeare's time! However, the area itself may have contained roe deer.

Soon after entering the village, food and drink may be taken at the Boars Head on your right. This interesting pub has been in the ownership of Hampton Lucy church since the first building was erected some 450 years ago (the present building is about 100 years old). Proceed straight on to reach the Church of St Peter ad Vincula which is known as 'the Cathedral in the Country' and is well worth a visit. St Peter ad Vincula is 'St Peter with chains' referring to the chains with which St Peter was bound by Herod Agrippa.

Now continue past the church and the primary school, to a

The magnificent church at Hampton Lucy

23

junction, where you turn right towards Charlcotte and Warwick. After 100m, you come to a river bridge ❹ – don't cross it but take the track on the left just after the last house. Go through the gate but, immediately before you reach the house in front of you, look for a public footpath sign and steep narrow track up to the left. Follow the obvious track round to the right as it levels out to present us with, perhaps, the most impressive views of the walk above the river.

You are in trees initially and then a gate takes you out to the edge of the field (don't take the path on the right that continues through the trees). As the trees obscure the views to the right our eyes are drawn over left towards the familiar landmark on the Welcombe Hills.

Ignore a sign to take you back into the woods but, rather, stay on the edge of the field where the going is easier. This ridge above the river really is a highlight of walking in South Warwickshire.

Eventually you come to a stile that gives access to a sitting area. Our route is *not* here but it is still a good place to take a break on the bench. (Our party managed to lose a black pearl from a necklace in this area – if found please return via the publisher!). Continue on the same line quickly passing a single old gnarled oak on your left. Continue into the next field where the way ahead is marked by a line of four trees that are across the field rather than close to its edge. Pause at the last of these to pick out the spire at Sherbourne. Further right, but in the distance, is the tower of St. Mary's Church at Warwick.

Carry on the same line until you are almost at the highest point. Then turn off to the right, on a line with the church at Sherbourne, and swing left around a bushy area within which is a trig point (though you probably will not see it unless you search!). Our route is reasonably well marked as we traverse round, really giving the impression of a circular walk heading for home. The path (now differing from the O.S. map) meanders for about 300m and then takes you through trees as you finally descend, awkwardly, to the road. Turn left, climb for 100m, and turn right into the drive of Daisy Hill Farm and follow it as it bends round, right, towards the buildings.

Just before reaching the farm, a path crosses the drive with stiles to left and right. Take the stile on the left and quickly come to another one, beyond which, you turn right. Follow the edge of the field into a corner. Turn left in front of two gates for 10m, and take the stile right into the next field. Turn sharp left and stick close to the hawthorn hedge on your left, passing a stone trough to take the stile to the right of the gate ahead.

Start to climb again, for a short distance, until the hedge turns sharp left. At this corner, our route is right, on a track across the field towards a hedge end, 100m ahead. Just before the hedge end, turn left and follow the low hedge and ditch on your left, and notice the roof of a red brick house becoming visible ahead. Follow the route as it goes through a gap by a telegraph pole, onto a drive, bear right and continue to follow it, in front of two cottages, until you reach the road. Turn right along this.

✪ At the junction, cross straight over the main Stratford-Warwick Road into Sandbarn Lane. ❺ Follow this until the road swings sharp right at a wall, in front of a green roofed property. Leave the road, by a stile, at the left-hand end of the wall behind the chevrons. Pass quickly beyond the end of the garden to a waymarked tree (the facing waymark was missing when we last walked, but there was still one on the opposite side of the tree). Go through the gap in the hedge and carry on, for 10m, to a corner by a garden shed. Pause for a moment and look diagonally right, to pick out the church tower at Snitterfield, which is our general line. As you proceed across the field, the cedar tree to the left of the church tower gives the more accurate line to a kissing gate. *Very carefully (and very patiently!)* cross straight over what can be a fast and busy road, and take the cycle lane through the gap. Turn left behind the mound. Beyond the gate carry straight on along the road parallel to the by-pass. After 200m, carry straight on at a junction, and continue until you reach the war memorial on your left. Pause for a moment and read the inscription on the stone seat, as our whole day is visible beneath us. Turn right, down White Horse Hill, via the village shop, and so, back to the start in the square.

Snitterfield is known as a village that really missed out on fame, being the birthplace of Shakespeare's father. He is supposed to be buried in the churchyard. The church, itself, dates back to Norman times.

5

Snitterfield and Claverdon

Distance: 8½ miles/13.5 km.
Features: Some interesting villages, rolling countryside and fine views.
Terrain: Moderate.
Maps: Landranger 151; Pathfinder 998/976.
Car Parking: In the village square.
Public Transport: Stratford Blue service 24 from Stratford. Alight at the Foxhunter Inn.
Refreshments: Pubs in Snitterfield and Claverdon (with a nice garden).
Start: Snitterfield (G.R.213597).

START in the village square and, with your back to the Foxhunter Inn, turn right up the hill towards the Snitterfield Arms, passing the Methodist church on your left and the school on your right. Go past the Highfield Close turning and, after a few metres, come to an electricity pole on the right. Take the public footpath between the houses. Cross the stile and enter the playing fields, keeping close to the hedge on the left. Proceed in the same direction to the corner and take the stile on the left. The well-walked path takes you gradually over to the right-hand hedge and, about 20m before the far side of the field, take the stile and footbridge on the right.

Keep to the edge of the field with the hedge on your left. As the ground gradually rises at the next corner, cross the rough gravel track and take the stile in the same direction going through two fields but this time with the hedge on your right.

This lovely raised position gives good views to the east towards the town of Warwick. At the next stile, carry on the same line with the hedge on your right. As a point of reference some power lines begin to cross our path from the left. You will also notice an island of trees in the field on your left. As you reach the end of the field, follow the hedge round to the left into the corner and, when it appears that you can go no further, take the stile on the right into the trees. Follow the well marked path through the trees, with the golf course on your left, for about 200m. When you emerge at the edge of the field the path continues straight across to trees on the opposite side (but when we last walked it crops forced us to go round the edge).

Take the obvious track, on the same line, straight down with the hedge on the right. This is a delightful spot, the only regret being that no public path exists to the right for further exploration.

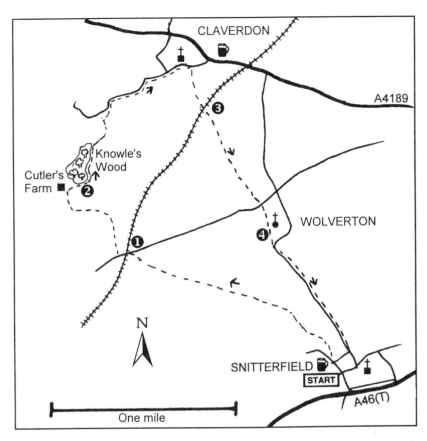

Continue straight on until you swing right and reach the road. ❶
Turn left under the railway bridge. Ignore the stile immediately under
the bridge and carry on for another 100m and take the small gate on the
right. Take a line straight across the field towards and slightly left of the
two green gates on the far side, via three large trees. Take another
newish gate to the left of these trees and then go slightly left to rejoin the
hedge at a point about 150m ahead. Follow the hedge for about 100m
and go through a gate.

Take the wooden footbridge and another gate and follow the path
uphill, close to the hedge on the right. There is a 'blasted' oak tree ahead
on the ridge. Although there are numerous other routes around, ignore
them all and carry straight on for 200m. When you are near the oak tree,
go through a gap into another field and turn left. Initially keep close to
the hedge on your left but then bear right as the path separates away
from it and follows a meandering course (though still with the hedge
visible over to the left).

Follow this for about 200m and on reaching the far end of the field
turn left at a waymarker and go through a gate on the right and over a
bridge to reach a tarmac drive. Turn right, towards Cutlers Farm. ❷

27

Above the farm, the obvious gap between the trees of Austy Wood and woodland to the right is visible from many parts of the south of the County.

Continue up the drive, crossing the cattle grid having passed the ancient oaks, to admire the imposing farmhouse. 100m beyond the cattle grid, take the gate on the right (with a single tree) opposite a water trough. Follow the line of the hedge up towards Knowles Wood with the hedge on your left. On reaching the wood, turn right. Pause for a moment and look back. Even the slight climb from the road opens up all sorts of views.

After 200m walking close to the woods on your left, arrive at a stile, with a gate a few metres further on. Turn left over the stile into the woods and follow the path through the trees but with the field edge only 50m or so to your right. As you near the edge of the woodland the path begins to descend but, 20m before you emerge from the trees, there is a waymark post indicating a right-hand turn which you take.

After 50m, leave the woods. Take the path down to the left, keeping the woodland on your left. 100m after leaving the woods, take the path left through a gap in the trees. This is an important turn. Follow the path for about 300m with the wood about 50m to your left. Just as you begin to get annoyed, as you feel the path is not going anywhere and the ground is a bit rough, you come to a T-junction in the path. Turn left here with a large jungle of brambles for company and with a waymark sign into the woodland again. After 50m, cross a footbridge and see a newish folly on your left.

Follow the narrow path as it climbs, with the screen of firs on your left and a view of a half-timbered house on the right. Cross a drive and descend some steps to a road. Turn right, to Tattle Bank

At the top of the road, come to a junction at a grass triangle. Turn left. Keep on the left-hand verge around this sharp bend and then cross over the road to face the on-coming traffic. You will quickly pass the entrance to the 'Woodside' B&B. Continue on in the same direction. At a junction, where Langley Road becomes Church Road, carry straight on into the village of Claverdon. There is an interesting cottage with an outside lantern on the left at the corner of Glebe Road.

Follow the road round to pass the church and, 50m beyond the church, look for a right-hand turn into Park Farm Drive.

At this point, if you wish for a pub stop, the Red Lion is a short distance further on but you must return to Park Farm Drive after refreshment to resume.

Follow the farm drive down for 50m to a gate and take the stile to the right with the waymark sign. From the stile, take a diagonal line right, to the far corner of the field, on a line roughly parallel to the power lines on the right. At the corner, go through the gate and note the little pond as a point of reference. Bear right, passing around a small mound on your left. Now walk with a hedge on your right and the small pond over to your left.

At the end of the field go through a gap, cross a farm track and continue in the same direction, still with the hedge on your right. This will bring you a railway line ❸ which you cross *very carefully*. Keep on the same line with a single red brick building on your left for reference.

About 100m before you reach the trees at the far side of the field, look diagonally left and take a faint path to a stile. Cross the stream, via a little concrete footbridge, and take a line straight up the field with a waymarked arrow. Ascend, via a curving track and crossing two stiles, to the ridge-line above the village of Wolverton with an attractive piece of woodland to the left.

Go past the big oaks on your left and, as the ground levels out at the top of the hill, you can just make out the church belfry at Wolverton. ❹

Pause and look back towards Claverdon with its church. At the road, don't cross to the stile, but turn right on the tarmac for 200m, until you reach the building on the left. Before the building, take the left-hand turn onto Manor Farm Drive.

This drive takes us above the village that, although nice, does not offer any facilities. We arrive quickly at the back of the church, with its distinctive weather vane. Do not go to the church but rather carry straight on the same line as a group of cottages, with an assortment of chimney pots, comes into view. Here, the track joins the road to Snitterfield. Turn right.

Follow the road up to the brow of the hill and then begin the descent into the village. Look straight ahead to the ridge that is the route of our outbound journey. About 20m down the hill there is a green gate on the left. Pause for a moment. Look hard over to the right for a glimpse of the Church tower at Snitterfield.

Wolverton Church with its wooden tower

This undulating road now pleasantly proceeds for a mile or so, to the village sign from where a more close-up view of the Church may be had. The Church dates back to the 1100s.

Descend the hill past the Bowling Club, and follow the road sharp right at a bridge. You are quickly back in the village square at the end of a memorable day.

6

Wilmcote and Aston Cantlow

Distance: 7½ miles/12 km.
Features: Classic Shakespeare countryside. Black and white buildings, a section of canal and some lovely woodland paths.
Terrain: Undulating. Easy walking with one or two minor climbs.
! A couple of parts can be very muddy so it might be wise to reserve this walk to a settled dry period.
Maps: Landranger 151; Pathfinder 997.
Car Parking: Roadsides in the village.
Public Transport: British Rail to Wilmcote. Turn left on leaving the station and walk to the canal bridge. Just before the bridge take the stile on the right, opposite the private drive to 'Station House'. Then start reading from ★ below.
Refreshments: Pubs in Aston Cantlow and Wilmcote.
Start: Wilmcote village (G.R.164581)

WITH your back to the Mary Arden Inn, proceed straight up the road opposite, passing Mary Arden's house on your left.

Mary Arden, daughter of Robert Arden of Aston Cantlow, was the mother of William Shakespeare.

When you reach the canal bridge take the stile on the left, opposite the private drive to 'Station House'.

★ Descend to the towpath of the Stratford-upon-Avon Canal and walk with the water on your *left* – these directions make less interesting reading if you manage to start along the canal in the wrong direction! Pause for a moment to read the British Waterways information board.

After less than a mile, cross the first bridge ❶. This is another excellent example of the split bridges that allowed the horses tow-lines to pass through and are typical of our canal walks in this area.

Cross the stile and turn right on a line parallel to, but a few metres away from, the canal. After 50m, cross a stile and carry on in the same direction for 250m, passing under power lines, to a gap in a thorn hedge and waymark post on the left. Take a diagonal line left, uphill, away from the canal, making for the highest point on the hill ahead. The route is not well marked but a low waymark post *en route* is a help. When you reach the highest point look for a stile in the hedge which is then about 50m ahead.

Pause at the stile for a moment. Ahead, on the horizon, are Round Hill and Bannam's Wood which are visited on our Henley West route. Follow the horizon round to your left. The woodland to the south-west is Withycombe Wood which is part of our return journey.

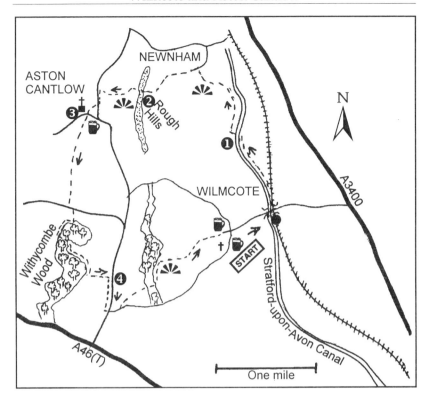

Leaving Wilmcote on the Stratford Canal

Anne F Wills

Descend, on the same line, towards the hamlet of Newnham, with the hedge on your left. Cross the little wooden footbridge at the bottom of the field and carry on in the same general direction. Cross a further two stiles, via a pump (presumably the old village pump) and concrete water trough (to the right), to a lane. Turn right and then quickly left at the junction. Keep bearing round to the left, then right, passing Ardencroft on your right and Lambs Cot (with well). After leaving the houses follow the farm track sharp left, on a line between two hedges (don't be tempted by two gates that are straight on).

After about 400m, the track turns sharp right across the field. (*If you look at the O.S. Map you will see that from this point the path into Aston Cantlow is not shown as a right of way. However, it is clearly well-used by walkers and riders and will not, we trust, cause any problems.*) This important turn is opposite a single large green and white building about 100m over to your left. After about 300m you are joined by a hedge on your right. The track becomes less pronounced and after another 250m you arrive at a gap in the hedge (marked by a large tree). You are now at the top of the escarpment known as the Rough Hills ❷.

Go through the gap and follow a track that can be muddy at times. After leaving the muddy section the track, now with a hedge on the right, swings right, then left, then right again through a hedge gap and forward towards houses. When you arrive at the road opposite 'Fairfield', turn left.

Follow the road through Aston Cantlow village as it bears round to the left and past the telephone box. Opposite the half-timbered village hall is the Kings Head and a welcome lunch stop! ❸

Turn right at the pub, into Church Lane and into the churchyard, via the lych-gate at Ivy Cottage. Fork left, immediately, at the waymark sign and, after 50m, leave the churchyard at a stile. Carry on, narrowly, to a footbridge by a willow and take the stile into the field. Take a line, slightly left of a mid-point in the hedge opposite, to a stile. Cross the road and proceed straight on up the farm drive with public footpath sign and hedge on your right. After 200m, pass under some power lines and look up left to the village of Wilmcote and our destination.

At a plantation, the main route turns sharp right but our route carries straight on here, with a waymark post and hedge to the right. Enjoy the views to the left and right of low wooded hills which are typical of the Arden countryside.

Take the stile at the corner of the large field, to emerge at the road. Turn left and, after 100m, take the gate on your right and ascend the path forward, directly to the edge of the wood, where you bear right with the wood on your left. Proceed to a gate and so into the trees. The route is pretty obvious, though it can be very muddy, with a barbed-wire fence on your left and the edge of the field just a few metres to your right. Ignore the right hand turn at a hollow tree.

Follow the path as it bears left, away from the fields, and starts to climb, finally emerging from the trees. Turn right along the edge of the wood. A group of white cottages in a stand of Scots Pines appears over to our left. We will walk past these presently but, meanwhile, continue to a gap. As a hedge joins from the left, turn left, and follow it (on your right) down to the cottages and the road ❹.

Turn right and continue past the Billesley Manor Hotel (where Shakespeare wrote *As You Like It*. Follow the wall to a junction where you turn left (by a line of poplars) on the road to Wilmcote. To the right of the grand entrance to the Hotel, take the hidden stile and proceed diagonally right, taking a line to the left of both the stone barn and the newer house beyond.

Interestingly, as we make our way across the field, on our left is the water-filled moat that is part of the original manor site. Take the stile just to the right of the end telegraph pole into a field and turn right, following its edge, with the hedge on the right.

At the bottom of the field, cross a little footbridge and turn sharp left. Proceed for 100m until the end pole of a power line is seen on the left. Turn sharp right here, across a narrow strip of land, to a stile and ascend on the same line, beneath the wires into the wood.

The ascent is steep and can be muddy but the short, sharp, shock is quickly rewarded at the top with views over towards Stratford-upon-Avon. With the spire of Trinity Church, the resting-place of William Shakespeare, visible beneath the Cotswold

Mary Arden's house, Wilmcote

escarpment, turn left, and follow the obvious track along the edge of the wood to a T-junction. Take the stile and footbridge straight ahead into a field.

Take a line that climbs diagonally right across the field to the right-hand end of the hedge in front of you and, to a stile at the high point. You are now in an area of all-weather gallops. *Watch out carefully for galloping horses!*

Cross the stile and bear slightly right for 50m, with the hedge on your left, to a track. Turn left and then immediately right through a gap in the white railings.

Carry on, in the same direction, down towards Wilmcote, with the tall hedge and trees on your right. This is an obvious wide path. Follow this all the way to the village and, as you arrive at some modern houses in a cul-de-sac (Swans Close), cross straight over the road and take the gated lane ahead between the house and hedge. This is Foxes Lane and, after 100m, you emerge on the road opposite the Sports and Social Club. Turn right and follow the road, past the Masons Arms, as it curves round to the right and back to our starting point.

7

Wellesbourne and Ashorne

Distance: 8½ miles/13.5 km.
Features: Riverside walking. Interesting villages, including the estate village of Charlecote.
Terrain: Fairly flat.
Maps: Landranger 151; Pathfinder 998; Explorer 205.
Car Parking: Rear of the Kings Head.
Public Transport: Stagecoach services X18 (Stratford/Coventry); Alight at the Kings Head, Wellesbourne.
Refreshments: Pubs in Wellesbourne and Ashorne.
Start: Facing the wrought iron gates outside St. Peter's Church, Wellesbourne, to the rear of the Kings Head pub in Church Street (G.R.278556).

ENTER the churchyard via the gate on the left, at a waymarker and follow the wall round to the left of the church. At the far end of the churchyard take the small blue gate and follow the narrow path to the footbridge. Descend the steps on the far side and turn right. Follow the path alongside the River Dene under the road, via a kissing gate. Our route is now obvious and well marked as it follows the left-hand bank (crossing a private drive en route) to reach the road opposite Charlecote Park ❶. The distinctive spire of Charlecote church is occasionally visible, diagonally right.

A section of the River Dene between Charlecote and Wellesbourne

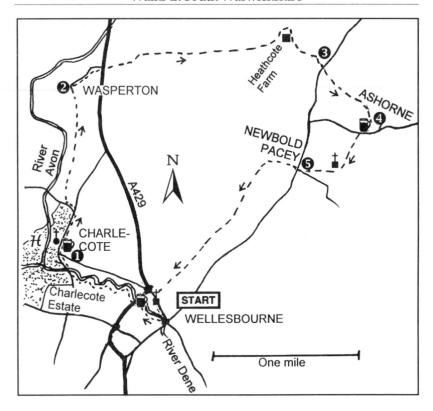

It is possible, by turning left at the road and then right after a short distance, through a hedge, to make an 'out and back' walk of one mile across the estate where Shakespeare was said to have poached for game.

At the road, turn right and cross the attractive stone bridge. Follow the road past the garden centre (refreshments available), and note the tumble down stile on the right (it is more impressive than it looks – push down the bar!). There is also an indication that Shakespeare had interests other than poetry.

Carry straight on past the Charlecote Pheasant Hotel and St. Leonard's Church and take the left-hand turn to Hampton Lucy. The deer in the park are normally visible in this corner. The large church tower at Hampton Lucy comes into view. *A closer look will be found in Walk 4.* Cross to the right-hand side of the road and, after 100m, note the Charlecote village sign and cross the little stream marked by a low brick wall and rails. Beyond the rails turn right and take the stile by the double gates. Follow the edge of the field towards a single red barn with the stream on your right. (After only 50m you pass a concrete inspection tank as a point of reference).

At the end of the first field, cross the stile and turn immediately left, keeping close to the fence. After 100m, at the trees, turn right to again follow the edge of a field. Pass a pond with two islands on your left and take the stile, with waymarker and, after 50m, go through a kissing gate (ignoring a stile on the left).

Walk forward and after just over 100m cross a metal footbridge and follow a wide track as it swings right towards the village of Wasperton. Stay on this well-defined track as the village comes into view ❷, with the church spire beyond. The ridge up to our left is part of the route for the Snitterfield-Hampton Lucy walk, which provides splendid views across the Avon Valley. Pass another popular angling pool on your right and, as you reach the tarmac road in the village, follow it round to the right.

Proceed on past the post and telephone boxes on your right and then take the next right-hand turn into the drive of a single house (College Farmhouse). Proceed for 50m but, before reaching the house, take the stile on the left. Carry on in a straight line behind the houses until you reach the road. At the road turn left and, after only 20m, cross the road *very carefully* turning right onto an unnamed farm drive.

After 200m the track swings left, then shortly right. After about three-quarters of a mile pass a farm and then about 200m further on the route goes straight on at a gap in the hedge rather than the more obvious route round to the left.

At a double gate the route up to Heathcote Farm is very obvious, the house occupying an impressive position (there is a sign that stops riders at this point). Continue up towards the house and turn left in front of it (If you haven't done so already, pause and look back). Immediately beyond the cattle grid the drive is private, so by the old 10m.p.h. sign, turn right into a field. Follow the metal fence on your right for 50m to a gap and a tiny waymark sign on a post.

Turn right, through the gap, and then take a diagonal line left across the field. We are reassured by a waymark sign on the far side. The way does split in two here but our route takes the gap to the right with an old sluice gate to your left, beneath some willows, and a boxed tap on your right. Take a direct line across the field, via the telegraph pole and, on the far side, turn left and then immediately right to continue to follow the edge of the field for a further 150m, until you reach a gap.

Go through the gap and turn left with the hedge on your left and some farm buildings straight ahead. After 100m, arrive at a corner and go through the gap onto the road and turn right ❸. A post box is visible about 50m, up on the left-hand side and, just beyond this, our route is marked. We leave the road at right-angles on the left via a stile and take a line to the right-hand end of the red brick buildings ahead. The fencing in this area is temporary and changeable but there is a stile in the middle of the field that indicates our line.

Keep on line for the right-hand end of the building and we are reassured by two stiles, close together, with waymarkers. After the second stile take a line diagonally left, away from the hedge.

As you gradually climb, pause to look back at our route so far. Our route is confirmed by a waymarked stile, just to the right of the two large trees on the far side of this field. Go straight across the next field to another stile and waymarker. Go straight forward to reach and cross a stile and the village rooftops will quickly come into view. Descend into the village of Ashorne, via the allotments, to the road. Turn right and, after 100m, arrive at the very agreeable Cottage Tavern for refreshments. ❹

50m beyond the pub, the road swings sharp round to the right. Take a left turn here, across the gravel drive to a single wrought-iron gate and waymarker (the double gates are a private entrance).

Descend the well-walked path across the classic village cricket ground to the pavilion with its clock tower. Cross the little footbridge on its left and proceed straight on up the edge of the field beyond. Ignore the first stile on the right after 200m, but rather, continue up the well-worn path to the corner of the field and take the small gate ahead. Carry on the same line to enter the churchyard. Follow the path round to the right of the church (St. George's), and onto the tarmac drive and the hamlet of Newbold Pacey ❺.

Follow the drive as it curves round to the right between two white gateposts and left to join the main road with a pond on our left.

Cross straight over the road (with care), and continue up the 'White Oaks' drive with a white gate at its entrance. Carry straight on along the edge of the field on a fairly wide track. The tarmac ends but we continue straight on, just below field level, for 400m until the track turns sharp left. Follow the track, obviously, round to the left and it is soon lined with small trees. (As a point of reference there is a right-hand turn, with

The cricket ground at Ashorne

waymarker, shortly after the sharp left-hand turn, but our route is straight on).

We continue on the same line, enjoying occasional open views, with a large hawthorn hedge for company. Follow the path until it swings right to enter a field. Walk forward with a hedge on the right to join another enclosed track. After about 400m this swings right into a field. Turn sharp left and follow the edge of the field (hedge on left) for 100m to the corner of the field. Straight ahead are the green roofs of the horticultural research station at Wellesbourne, and beyond and above is the obelisk on the Welcombe Hills.

Carry straight on through the gap (in the same direction) into another field and after 40m reach a waymark post. Continue to follow the hedge as it turns sharp left along the edge of the field. Over to the right are the houses on the edge of Wellesbourne and, just beyond them, the church tower at our starting point.

Descend slightly into the corner of the field to a waymarker post. Go through the gap in the hedge here and carry on in the same direction into another field. Ahead now are power lines that cross your path. Go beneath them and follow the hedge to the corner of the field. Turn right and continue along the edge of the field with the hedge on the left, virtually beneath the power lines.

Go through a gap into another field and continue with the hedge on your left for 30m. After the hedge ends strike out across the field on the line of the power poles. On the far side of the field take the gap in the hedge, just to the left of the power poles. Bear left across the next field towards the new houses (leaving the power lines over to your right) in a general line with the church tower.

Cross the wooden footbridge and continue to follow the tarmac path alongside the houses to emerge at the road where you turn left.. Continue down to the junction at the big Shell garage, opposite the Kings Head. Cross straight over into Hoppers Lane, to the left of the pub, and so back to the start in Church Street.

8

Stratford-upon-Avon Three-Ways Walk

Distance: 12½ miles/20 km.
Features: Picturesque riverside section. A disused railway line
(The Greenway) with much still in evidence of the railway's past.
Interesting villages with many black & white buildings.
Terrain: Easy. Mostly flat on paths and tracks.
Maps: Landranger 151; Pathfinder 998/997; Explorer 205.
Car Parking: Greenway car park (G.R.196541). See map below.
Public Transport: British Rail and numerous bus services to
Stratford-upon-Avon. To reach the starting point see the map
below.
Refreshments: Pubs and cafés in Stratford; pub in
Welford-on-Avon.
Start: At the Information Boards on the far side of the Greenway
Car Park (G.R.196541). See the map below.

W ITH your back to the information boards (these are well worth a
look), facing the by-pass, make for the top right-hand corner of
the car park and take the path which runs parallel to the road,
until you reach the river. Turn left under the road bridge and cross the
river via the footbridge. Turn right on the far bank on the Avon Valley
Way. Continue for a few minutes until a picturesque lock is reached,
one of several that were constructed in the 1970s when the River Avon
was re-opened to traffic after having become unnavigable in the middle
of the last century.

Follow the path as it
ascends a steep zigzag up to
the left through woods, until it
finally emerges in a field. Turn
right and follow the edge of
the field in a delightfully
raised position above the
river.

Follow the edge of the field
as it gently descends towards
the river, until an old railway
bridge comes into view, with a
metal superstructure above it.
This, now disused, railway
line has been converted into
`The Greenway', a walking

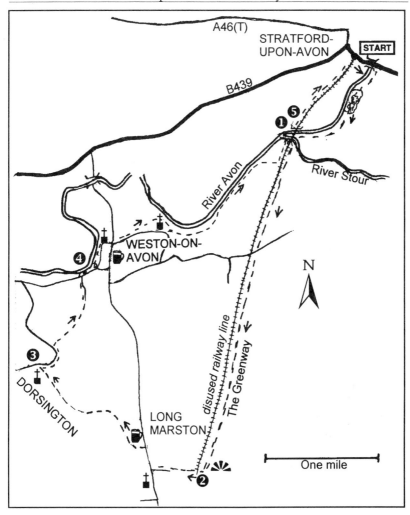

and cycling way, opened in 1989, that runs south from Stratford-upon-Avon to Long Marston, a distance of almost five miles.

The Greenway runs along the old Honeybourne Railway, built by the Oxford, Worcester and Wolverhampton Railway in 1859, and absorbed by the Great Western Railway in 1908. It was closed in 1979.

The Greenway is a haven for wildlife, many trees and bushes having grown up alongside it since it was closed to rail traffic. There are many fruit trees, a consequence of the large amounts of fruit that were brought along the line from Evesham to the Birmingham market.

Follow the path round to the left in front of the brick archways and take the small wooden kissing gate. 25m further on you come to a brick tunnel beneath the railway. *Do not* go underneath, but take the stile on

41

the right and climb the short slope to the old railway. Turn left and follow the old raised railway track.

After a short distance you cross the River Stour. It is at this point that the Stour joins the Avon ❶.

After about a mile you will come across a railway cottage on your left and just beyond it some upright white-painted concrete sleepers guarding the path. You will notice the Corsican pines at the Milcote picnic site ahead. These were planted when new platforms at Milcote were constructed after the railway had been taken over by the GWR in 1908.

Pass through a second set of concrete sleepers and then soon reach Milcote. Here you will notice the remains of railway platforms. It is easy to imagine how these old platforms were once a station. Cross the road and continue straight ahead where you will see further remains of by-gone railway activity. The picnic site occupies the original site of the stationmaster's garden.

From here The Greenway takes on a rather more remote aspect. The path narrows as bushes and trees close in.

Pass a third set of sleepers. You will see the Cotswold escarpment ahead and Meon Hill to the left. The village of Long Marston begins to appear on your right.

Continue for about 3 km/1¾ miles until, shortly after crossing a private road, you reach a fourth set of concrete pillars ❷. Here turn right and leave the old railway, passing Railway Cottage on your left. This road is part of the 'Heart of England Way'. Continue until you reach the T-junction at Long Marston by a telephone box and 'Heart of England' sign.

Turn right. After 50m, just past the chapel, turn left along a path that swings right and passes between houses to reach a stile..

Site of the old railway station at Milcote

Take the stile into a field and turn sharp left along the hedge.

Cross two stiles and carry straight on for 150m. Turn sharp right along the hedge and over a stile. Keep tight to the hedge (on your right) and cross three fields until you come to a footbridge. Pause on the footbridge for a moment.

Head for the nearest telegraph pole diagonally on your left (and waymarked). Carry on the same line for 300m occasionally looking back towards the bridge for reference. Pass through the remains of an old hedge that crosses the middle of the field – if you are strictly on course you should see another waymark on a low tree. Now aim for a stile in the far left corner of the field and a wooden footbridge. Cross this and continue on the same bearing, soon following a muddy track but leaving it when it swings away to the right at a gate. Keeping a hedge and stream on your left pass through several fields to reach a stile taking you onto a road. ❸

Now leaving the Heart of England Way turn right. (The village of Dorsington is left but has no facilities although it has a number of interesting buildings and is worth further exploration). After the first left-hand bend (by a house) carry on for 120m to a gap in the hedge on your right with a stile and public footpath sign (*before* reaching the next house). Carry on diagonally left, leaving a large barn on your left. Continue to the far left-hand corner of the field. Cross two stiles and carry straight on through three fields, following the hedge on your right.

In the third field Hunt Hall Farm buildings will appear. Entering a fourth field through a gate make for the right-hand corner of the buildings and a waymark sign. Go through the gate and join the main farm track. Turn left and follow the track, soon surfaced, passing to the right of barns and later some chalet-bungalows, for about half a mile to the road.

Turn left. After 300m, opposite the entrance to a large house on the brow of the hill, turn right into the trees at an easily missed kissing gate. Look right for a moment for a good view of Welford-on-Avon. Descend steeply to the river. Turn right.

Carry on for a few hundred meters until, passing fir trees on your left, you enter a caravan site. At the entrance to the site, turn left and then immediately right at The Mill House, then right again at a Severn-Trent sub-station, passing some fine thatched cottages to arrive at the church. Carry straight on (east) up to the High Street and at the road junction enjoy a pint at the Bell Inn ❹. The village is noted for its variety of black and white buildings.

Cross straight over the road and narrowly continue between two cottages. An Avon Valley Way sign shows the way.

Pass along a narrow field, then between fences to reach a tarmac drive. Continue along this for a few metres, then go left through a gap in the hedge and along an enclosed path (this runs parallel to the drive for 50m and emerges in the same place). Reaching the drive again, turn left (by River Bank) and pass Pear Tree Close to descend a path to the River Avon. Stay close to it and do not be tempted by a path to the right. After about 250m the path swings away from the river to emerge onto a lane (Avon Valley sign here).

Turn left, towards the church tower (somewhat obscured in summer by trees), passing thatched cottages and a telephone box, and swinging left to pass the church on your left. Carry straight on, passing the Weston-on-Avon Severn-Trent building on your left, on a clear, wide track. On reaching a facing hedge on the far side of the field look for a waymarked post to take you left (behind the hedge and just before the track joins the farm drive) to join the river.

Follow the path round to the right as it runs parallel to the river. A large lock and weir are evident here (but less so with trees obscuring them in summer). Follow the meandering paths to turn left, just beyond the footbridge, to join the river again at a line of poplars. Now head back towards Stratford, passing many pollarded willows and with the attractive church spire of Shakespeare's resting place coming into view.

At a large willow and a wooden footbridge follow the waymarker as it takes you, at right-angles, away from the river and, in the corner of the field which is at the bottom of the bank of The Greenway, follow the path round to the left. Cross a footbridge ❺, turn left for 150m and then right under the arch. Turn immediately left at the stile to rejoin The Greenway and follow it towards Stratford. At the bridge with the metal superstructure overhead you can descend again and follow the river if desired – either way we are nearly home on familiar ground. Stratford racecourse is to the left and on the old railway there was a station here with an extra long platform for the masses of visitors expected on race days!

Timing your walk to arrive during a race meeting would make a spectacular end to the day. At the end of The Greenway you have a choice of three narrow paths beyond the barrier. Take the middle one and, all of a sudden we are back at the car-park.

9

Combrook and Lighthorne

Distance: 8½ miles/13.5 km.
Features: The wonderful Compton Verney Estate. The interesting, but very different, villages of Combrook and Lighthorne.
Terrain: Gentle rolling countryside.
Maps: Landranger 151; Pathfinder 998.
Car Parking: In the village, near the church.
Public Transport: Limited service Stagecoach 271/278/279 from Stratford/Leamington Spa to Lighthorne where you could start the walk.
Refreshments: Pub in Lighthorne
Start: The delightful village of Combrook, situated off the Wellesbourne to Kineton road, close to the Fosse Way (G.R.308517)
! This walk is best avoided after a long, wet spell, or when crops are at their full height.

OUR start is at the parish church of St. Mary and St. Margaret, with its ornate spire and interesting stone work. Face the church entrance, which lies at a junction, and take the road to the left (with a wagon wheel built into the wall on your left). Continue down the lane for about 100m, to the ornamental well at Chestnut House on the right. 50m beyond the well look for a waymarker on the right and ascend to a stile.

Carry on in the same direction (there is no obvious path), still climbing, moving gradually over towards the woodland on your left. After about 100m, and before reaching the far, left-hand corner of the field, look carefully for a stile and waymarker into the woods. (There is another stile right in the corner of the field that takes us onto the road and is NOT our route).

Before going into the woods, pause to look back over the roof-tops of Combrook, a delightful village. The way through the woods is obvious and a direct line takes you straight through. Ignore a track on the right after 150m which leads to the road via a gate. At the gap on the far side we get our first view of the lake at Compton Verney. This is a superb 'Capability Brown' landscaped estate. Look diagonally right here and if you are tall enough you may just pick out the tops of a pair of pillars that are near to the entrance to the house. These are our next objective and a waymark points a diagonal line to them ❶. However, if the path is cropped it may be easier to take an alternative waymarked path straight forward across the field to the road and turn right for a short distance, towards the acorn-topped pillars.

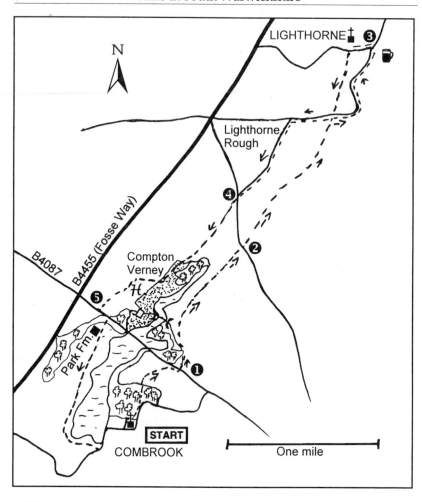

Turn left into the main entrance but, after only 20m, leave the drive onto the grass at a waymark post on the right and so onto a little wooden footbridge. Carry straight on across an avenue of Californian proportion pine trees, bearing slightly right to quickly arrive at the edge of a field.

Pause for a moment by the waymarked post. Over to the right is woodland, including a group of small fir trees. The waymarker leads us diagonally left. However, to pick up what is normally a well-ridden route walk straight on uphill for about 50m, towards the high point on the near skyline, before striking out diagonally left. (On a previous occasion we turned sharp right around the edge of the field for 25m, towards fir trees, and then sharp left into the field to pick up the route.) Anyway, be bold and head off across this large field.

Over to the left water comes into view about 150m away and we find ourselves gradually getting closer and closer to the woods that shield the water. Our line eventually joins the trees as they thin out at a gap and a waymarked post.

The route here is less obvious (depending on the time of the year) but, after about 300m in the same direction, a pond becomes visible over to the left and, sometimes, the more obvious and well-ridden route is slightly closer to the edge of the field on your left. Anyway, continue parallel to the edge of the field and aim just to the left of the single tree on the horizon. A tarmac road comes into view over to the left: continue straight on until you reach this road ❷. This point has waymarkers on both sides of the road and also a red triangular motorists sign. Here the road dips down left to a red brick bridge about 100m away.

The magnificent bridge across Capability Brown's lake at Compton Verney

Cross over at the public bridleway sign and carry on in the same direction. You are soon joined by a hedge on the right and, about 100m after leaving the road, follow the track right, through a gap in the hedge, and then immediately left. Follow the hedge on your left for a further 50m and then strike out again straight across the field in the same direction, climbing slowly and obviously. As the farm at Hillfields becomes visible on the right the ground levels out. Eventually, cross straight over the farm drive, beneath the power lines, onto a narrow track with a hedge on the left, a metal gate 100m ahead and a bridleway sign.

Continue along the grassy track until drawing level with the farm complex on the right and take the large metal gate by the newer detached brick house on the left. Just beyond the house, on the drive, turn left and follow it to the road, with Dutch barn straight ahead. Turn right at the junction and follow it as it quickly swings round to the left and, eventually, down into the village of Lighthorne. Here you can refresh yourselves at the delightful and welcoming Antelope. ❸

Just beyond the pub turn left at the village green and immediately left again. You quickly pass the village pump on the right as a point of reference. Proceed until a junction is reached. Here the no-through road goes to the church but we turn left. Carry straight on, passing Northbrook House on the left and the end of the cottages on the right. Proceed until you reach the Severn-Trent building on the left. Cross the small, brick bridge over the brook and turn left, immediately, at the rather shabby pull-in place. Follow the track up through the trees to a gate.

Keep right, beyond the gate, onto more open ground, with brambles, and climb for 100m or so, until the ground becomes less steep and the route becomes more obvious. Proceed with a fence on the right for a further 200m to reach a stile on the right of a metal gate.

Cross the stile and proceed straight on, after perhaps pausing for a final time to look back over the village of Lighthorne. As the field narrows carry straight on towards the farm and familiar Dutch barn. Take a line to the right-hand end of the farm buildings to a gate next to the hedge that has arrows on either side, indicating the route. Pass straight through two gates and proceed to the road, where you turn right. Carry on until you reach a junction at a grassy triangle just before some woodland. Take the left-hand turn here, leaving the woods on your right.

Follow the road as it descends slightly and passes an area on the right known as Lighthorne Rough that is shielded by conifers. The view diagonally left from here includes the lines of tall pine trees that we enjoyed earlier at Compton Verney House. This area has a delightful open feeling, particularly on a frosty winter's day. At the road junction ❹ cross straight over onto a well-marked track with waymark sign. At this junction, if you follow with your eye left, over the red brick bridge, up to the horizon, the single tree marks our crossing point earlier in the day.

Proceed straight on at a gate with the house and lake at Compton Verney coming into view, with the three-span bridge creating a superb location. The house, itself, has undergone considerable restoration and now boasts an impressive public art gallery. There are few finer lake views. Follow the track as it swings round right, away from the house, to join a farm drive that, in turn, swings sharp left to eventually join the road at the gate house (Compton Verney Lodge). At the road ❺, turn left and follow it downhill, crossing onto the right-hand side.

As the road levels out at the bottom of the hill look for the entrance to Park Farm and turn right into it (opposite the Compton Verney sign). Carry straight on up the drive, past the left-hand turn that would take you to the house with the tennis court. Just as you arrive at the cottages don't cross the cattle grid at the slow sign but leave the drive diagonally left onto the grass and go through a gate. (There is a 'Private' notice but this does not apply to this public footpath).

After 30m, turn left at the footpath and fishing signs and strike out across the open parkland towards two Scots pines by the lake. As we make progress across here, aim towards the right of the two Scots pines and be reassured by a waymark post. When you pass here the old (ancient!), wooden waymark post, keep left on the level ground towards the water rather than starting to climb. Take the wooden gate, or the kissing gate, that are beside an unusual wooden, slatted ramp.

The lakeside path here, with its fishing pegs, is well maintained. The path narrows as we approach the village between wooden rails. Don't be tempted off to left or right but follow the path down, over the stream and quickly up to the road (our outward route lies up the hill, straight over the road). Passing through a gate look over to the right for peacocks and peahens. When last walked there was an albino peacock with them. Turn right, on familiar ground, back to the start at the parish church where you can sit down on the bench.

10

Ettington, Idlicote and Whatcote

Distance: 10½ miles/17 km.
Features: Fine views. Lovely villages of Halford and Idlicote.
Terrain: Moderate. Two climbs.
Maps: Landranger 151; Pathfinder 1021; Explorer 205.
Car Parking: Roadside near the church.
Public Transport: Newmark Coaches service 270 from Stratford.
Alight at Ettington church.
Refreshments: Pubs in Ettington and Whatcote.
Start: The village church at Ettington (Holy Trinity and St. Thomas
of Canterbury) (G.R.266490), which is first right as you approach
the village from Stratford-on-Avon.

WITH your back to the lychgate, turn left and walk back to the main road at the give-way sign. Turn left again and proceed to the island passing the remains of the St Thomas à Becket church on the right. Here we turn left, very briefly, on the A429 towards Cirencester. Immediately cross over and, less than 50m on from the island, take the diagonal rising path on the right to the top of the embankment (waymark post). As you climb, look over to the left to the spire of the church at Aldermister. Take the old stile at the top and proceed left, on the tarmac track, towards Grove Farm.

Very quickly you can enjoy extensive views in all directions from this raised position, with our old friend Brailes Hill, with its wooded top, over to the left. Keep over to the right, through the farmyard (with old telephone box at time of writing), leaving the majority of the buildings over to your left. 200m beyond the buildings, take the left fork, with waymark sign. Almost immediately the twin radio masts on Ilmington Hill are visible ahead and slightly left. Very quickly, the woodland joins you on the right. Take the stile and waymark sign. Meon Hill is visible ahead with its macabre history, as is Bredon Hill, which is just to the right and beyond, above Evesham.

100m beyond the stile arrive at a gap where the woodland ends. Turn left, downhill, but keep close to the hedge on your left. Keep straight on at the obvious path as it enters the woodland (with the edge of the woods close on your left).

Emerge from the woods at three metal posts. Carry straight on in the same direction until, eventually, you drop down to a gate and lane ❶. Cross straight over by the double metal gates (and raised 'DOG' sign). This is an obvious wide path through the trees and, as the low pine trees finish on your left, join a track (waymark sign) and bear right. After a further 50m, take the left turn in the track (there is a waymark sign on

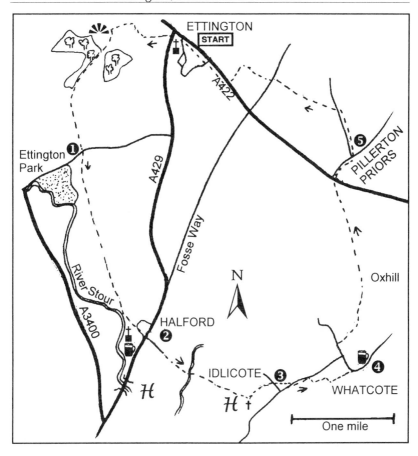

your right). The way is obvious here. Over to the right is the well-known Ettington Park Hotel (home for the Scottish European Cup soccer squad in 1996). The double track takes you on towards the village of Halford, with a wall on the right and a variety of trees giving a real parkland feel. A ha-ha (dry moat) guards the estate.

The way is well marked across open country and, unusually, passes between two large trees which are only three metres apart (waymark sign on right hand tree). The houses at Newbold are visible over to the right and, after another 400m, passes between another pair of trees. Pause for a moment and admire views in all directions, with Ilmington Hill visible, with masts, over to the right and the Hotel directly behind.

100m beyond this second pair, you arrive at the edge of the field. Go through the gap in the remains of a metal fence and turn sharp right (waymark sign). Keep close to the hedge on the right. Follow this to the corner, via a small dip, noted, at the time of writing, for its pile of assorted wood and metal, and turn left along the field edge. This is well walked.

51

We are now in a pleasant position above the River Stour. Don't be tempted down to the riverside – stay up high.

As the field narrows to about 30m, turn left at a waymark sign, away from the river, to a gate. The buildings of Halford village are now close at hand. Beyond the gate, take a line diagonally right, across the delightful Henry's Meadow, on a general line towards the church. Cross the stream via two gates and ascend up into the village. Take the gate at the left-hand edge of the long, white dwelling ahead.

❷ Halford is a delightful village, unseen from the main Fosse Way and well worth a visit, in its own right, to examine the old footbridge over the river that is parallel to the road. At the lane, beyond the gate, turn right and follow it round to the church. Continue round to the left in front of the church (Halford Forge). Proceed past the telephone box to the main road and cross straight over onto the Idlicote Road.

Continue until a T-junction is reached with the river for company on your right, with some interesting meadows and meanders. Cross straight over onto the farm track at a waymark sign and waymark post.

At the brow of the hill, in front of a double gate, follow the track round to the right. The houses at Idlicote are visible straight ahead at this gate and are our next objective. After a further 100m, turn left at a gap and faint waymark sign. Stay close to the hedge on your left and with, at the time of writing, a large pile of manure on your right.

Descend into the little valley and, when you reach the stream, take the metal gate on your left. Follow the edge of the stream for about 300m, passing an old plank footbridge. Eventually, just before reaching a gate, come to a more substantial footbridge with a handrail. Take this and bear left, then immediately right, to climb steeply (with minor stream / ditch on your left) through the trees to follow the hedge up left towards a barn – the roof of which comes quickly into view. Go to the left of the barn (waymark post) and just beyond cross straight over a track (waymark sign) and carry on with the hedge and trees on your left.

Go through a gate and follow the fence up into the village, climbing steeply to another gate. Pause here and look back at some impressive views. Idlicote is an interesting village – its location on the crest of a hill is impressive in itself. You pass through the grounds of Idlicote House with its fine gardens beautifully maintained (and a pleasant contrast to the state of decay that we encountered when we first walked here).

Carry on in the same direction on a track with an impressive stable yard on the right and a folly on the left. Beyond the stables is the estate house. Follow the track left, leaving St. James the Great, Idlicote ❸, on your right, until reaching the village pond and, on your left, an old petrol pump. At the junction, with a grass triangle, turn right and descend past 'Willow End' on the right, to the T-junction. Diagonally left, you can pick out the windmill at Tysoe, a highlight of Walk 12, and beyond it, the Edge Hill ridge. At the junction, turn left towards Whatcote. Very soon a farm complex comes into view on the right, with five long buildings and gable ends facing the road. Look for a right hand turn at the far end of these. Take the stile by the double gate into the yard and proceed through another gate. After another 50m, take the stile on the left and little footbridge just beyond another gate. Turn immediately right, along the edge of the field with the hedge on your right and, after 100m, look for a waymark post. Turn left here, at right angles, across the field and beneath power lines, as the village of Whatcote comes into view.

On the far side, follow the waymark sign right, keeping the hedge on your right for 50m, then turn left across the field again, to a gap on far side. Beyond this, a waymark post indicates your way diagonally right towards the church. Follow the telegraph poles and take a line to the left of the new brick-built property with oil tank. At the lane, turn left and proceed to the T-junction ❹. Our route is left but the 'Royal Oak', which is well worth a visit, lies a short distance to the right, the front of which was marked by an elm tree for many years. However, if you resist the temptation, turn left along the road, ignoring a footpath on the left.

After 400m, ignore the left turn back to Idlicote but rather carry on up the straight road ahead, for 30m beyond the junction and look for a waymark post and metal gate on the right. Leave the road here and make your way to Harrods Farm, with Oxhill Hill above and beyond. On the far side of this first field you reach a gap and, from here, take a direct line across to the farm, aiming just to the right of the buildings to arrive at a metal footbridge. Cross the bridge and gently ascend the field, with hedge on your right, to a gate beneath the telegraph lines. At the time of writing a 'House of Holland' container was on the left at the top of the rise, as a point of reference.

Go through another gate and follow the waymark sign, then proceed diagonally left across the next field beneath the power lines. On the far side, we are re-assured by a waymark sign on a telegraph pole. Enter the next field and follow the hedge line on your left. Leave this field, via a single plank over a ditch, and carry straight across the next field in the same direction, with the farm roofs becoming visible over to your right.

Cross the farm track and take the footbridge and stile straight ahead, keeping on the same line and aiming for a gap to the right of centre of the hedge that can be seen ahead. When the ground dips down look for a wooden footbridge at a mid-point in the hedge which will now have become visible ahead. Cross this and proceed straight forward, bearing slightly right to a gap (the one that you were aiming for earlier) and stile that offers a choice of two routes. Our line is straight on, to climb the hill towards Windmill Hill and the ridge at Pillerton Priors ahead, bearing slightly left, but to the right of the highest point of the hill, where the ridge line and hedge meet at the top.

About three-quarters of the way up the hill, a stile and waymark post come into view (about 100m left of some double metal gates). At the stile, the ground levels out. Pause and look back to enjoy views with a remote feeling. Carry straight on, as indicated, via a series of stiles and next to some old sheds, to the left of a dormer bungalow with a large conservatory, and so to the road junction with small grass triangle. Cross straight over and proceed straight on down the road with pavement. As the pavement ends, cross over and rejoin it on the left-hand side of the road. Follow it as it turns left at the junction (sign-posted Walton and Wellesbourne ❺. Follow this minor road as it rises slightly and leaves the speed restriction zone. The road levels out for 400m and then, begins to descend, as we are joined by some woods on our left. At the bottom, as the road levels out again, we are joined by a row of 11 poplar trees on the left, as the woods end.

100m beyond the poplars, go just past a pair of ancient wooden gates and waymark post on the right, and look for our route to the left at a metal gate and waymark post. Turn left through the gate and carry straight, on at right angles to the road, with a hawthorn hedge on your right.

After 400m, pass beneath power lines and on, beyond a pond and old willows on your left. Continue in the same direction, via some gates, and eventually into the yard of Brick Kiln Farm Stud. Keep right and continue along the tree-lined drive to the road. Cross straight over and enter the next field, making slightly left at a waymark sign, to a large oak tree and gap in the hedge on the far side.

Cross the little footbridge by the oak tree and continue, diagonally left, across the field (NOT sharp left to the gap) to a mid-point in the hedge. The wind pump marked on the newer O.S. map comes into view. Cross the double planks over the ditch at a gap and continue, with the wind pump more visible to our left, along the edge of the field with the hedge to the right.

On the far side of the field containing the wind pump, carry straight on to a line of conifers and to a gap with a wooden gate within them. Go through the gap but turn left *before* the gate, and so, narrowly, to 'The Chequers' car park and onto the road. Turn right. Cross the road onto the left-hand pavement and proceed, past 'The White Horse', into the village. As you arrive at the zebra crossing and Post Office at the far end of the village, the church tower comes into view. About 100m beyond the P.O. turn left into Church Lane and then right at the junction, and so, back to the start.

11

Radway, Ratley and Edgehill

Distance: 6½ miles/10.5 km.
Features: A walk packed with historical interest: Edgehill battle site, the manor at Arlescote, and General Haig's village of Radway. Lovely Horton Stone cottages and superb views.
Terrain: One steep climb.
Maps: Landranger 151; Pathfinder
Car Parking: Roadside in the village centre.
Public Transport: Nothing direct. However, limited service, Stagecoach X70/270/279 (Stratford/Banbury/Leamington Spa) will take you to Edgehill, Upton House from where a walk north along a minor road for about 2 km will bring you to Ratley and you could start your walk there.
Refreshments: Pubs in Warmington and Ratley.
Start: Radway G.R.372484.

THIS classic little journey is based on the two villages of Radway (below) and Ratley (above Edgehill). In addition to making an ascent of the scarp slope above the lunch stop at Warmington, it should also be noted that the second half is very undulating and explores some delightful, little known, valleys on the dip slope of the escarpment. This makes the walk both longer and more demanding than it would first appear but all the more interesting for it.

The start is at the T-junction in the middle of Radway with your back to the bus shelter. Turn right and proceed out of the village towards the B4086, passing the telephone box and post box on your right and an impressive stone wall. As you pass the final dwelling on the right, which is Townsend Farm, pause for a moment and look up to the top of the ridge on the right. There is a water tower in the trees to the left and the tower, which is the Castle Inn, over to the right, which is the point of our descent later on. As you proceed out of the village the Burton Dassett Hills (with Beacon), are visible straight ahead.

When you arrive at the T-junction ❶, turn right but only for 10m and then take the finger post on the left into the field. Proceed across the field in line with the ridge and furrow for 200m to a derelict building and pond. At the post turn sharp right and proceed uphill to a gap and stile in the hedge (well to the right of the white detached house). All you have done here is cut out a steep section of road walking. At the road turn left and proceed into the village of Arlescote, passing the detached white house on your left (Brickyard House). Arlescote is a village in harmony with its surroundings having a magnificent manor house of golden stone. ❷

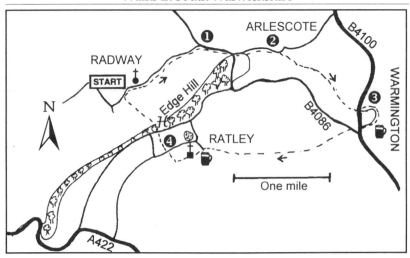

Immediately past the manor house (with tradesmen's entrance) on your left, in the centre of the village, the road curves round to the left. 100m beyond this left-hand bend (with the manor house still over to the left), there is a finger post on the right-hand side of the road. Leave the road here and go straight forward across the grass to a stile that leads onto a wide track/drive. Turn right here (in front of the pond), and then immediately left at the stile and waymarker.

Keep over to the hedge on the left, as we continue to skirt the foot of Edgehill and, at the end of this first field, take the stile and waymarker and 'pallet' footbridge.

The impressive manor house at Arlescote

56

Edgehill

The battle of Edgehill took place on 23 October 1642 and was the first battle of the English Civil War. The Royalists were led by Charles I, and Parliament by the Earl of Essex.

The King occupied the Edgehill Ridge on the 22nd. The Parliamentary army was down below in Kineton, having marched from Worcester in five days. The King's tent supposedly stood on the present site of the Castle Inn, having an uninterrupted view down the treeless slopes.

Cromwell took no part in the battle, being of little importance at that time, and keeping his 'head down' in Burton Dassett.

Each side lost approximately 3,000 of their 15,000 soldiers in an inconclusive encounter that fizzled out when the Royalists withdrew back up the hill and the Parliamentarians returned to Kineton. Tradition has it that the villagers 'heard' the battle some time later and that ghosts have been seen.

The Castle Inn was built 100 years after the battle by the architect Sanderson Miller of Radway Grange who was also responsible for designing the County Hall in Warwick and for planting the trees on the escarpment.

Continue in the same direction but bearing slightly left towards a metal gate and waymarker. Go through the gate and keep over to the right-hand side with a hawthorn hedge for company. After 75m, you come to a corner where the hedge turns sharp right. Here we proceed straight across the field, taking a line 100m to the right of the single tree. Eventually another waymarker comes into view on the far side of this large, normally cultivated field.

Go through the gap, turn left and then immediately right, to follow the edge of the field with the hedge on your left.

On the far side of this field turn left via a stile, go through a gap in the hedge, and then turn immediately right over a two-plank footbridge to return to the original line with the hedge on the right. Look on the far side of the field as it swings left to a stile with a large oak tree to its right (it is actually in front of it)

Cross the stile and Warmington comes into view. Follow the well-worn path across scrub and bear slightly right through a gate until you reach the road ❸. Cross over diagonally right and drop down a lane with 30m.p.h. signs, noting that the first house on the left is dated 1539. After 100m, go past Little Dene Cottage and Ivy Dene (with archway), and then turn right in front of Thimble Cottage. Pass the Methodist church on your left to emerge, eventually, at the junction with Church Hill by the post box. The Plough is just to the right here and the village pond is just down to the left and worth a look.

Turn right and pass the pub, climbing steeply out of the village with the village hall on the right. It is said that Cromwell marched his troops up this hill. As the road bends round to the right, take the obvious stone steps diagonally left, with handrail, up to the rear of the St Michael's Church and walk through the churchyard.

The twelfth century church is well worth a visit with many interesting features described in a leaflet available in the church. As you bear left to leave the churchyard look out for the war memorial on the right, perhaps speculating on why WH Haynes should have been a member of the 78th Winnipeg Grenadiers.

Turn left on the pavement and carry on for about 100m and then cross over, turn right and immediately take the right-hand turn to Edgehill (B4086).

Don't be tempted down the drive to Fir Tree Farm but rather look ahead to the left-hand side of the road to a large barn conversion with a particularly steep roof (and Velux windows) as a point of reference.

From here we get the impression that we are turning for home and are now more level with the Burton Dassett Hills which are over to our right.

200m beyond the barn conversion, look for a waymarker through a gap on the left, just before a gate. (The path also continues on the right-hand side of the road). Turn left here and leave the road and, after 100m, go through the gate with waymarks and take a diagonal line downhill on a general line with the radio mast on the far ridge. Don't be tempted with the tracks off to the left. Go straight on for 50m (unpromisingly), until a stile comes into view just beyond a power pole at the bottom of the slope. Beyond the stile, look for a gap in the hedge on the far side of this large field (on the same line), by a large tree. Go straight across the field to the gap and carry straight on through it in the same direction. We are generally parallel to the telegraph lines over to our right.

At the weekend, the gun club nearby will be obvious. Continue on the same line until you reach large, double metal gates on the far side of the field. Take the stile to the right of the gates and then proceed up the wide, grassy track between two lines of trees.

Follow the track as it bends round to the right. As the trees finish on the right, look for the double metal gates on the left. Go through these and, ignoring the Macmillan Way waymarks pointing to the right, take a line straight up the hill, parallel to the hedge that is 30m over to your left. Climb steadily uphill to a telegraph pole, stile and an equestrian-type fence at the top. Pause and look back.

Drop down into a secondary little valley in the general direction of the power lines, at the bottom of which we pass an overgrown pond on our left (waymarker on a post). High up to the right is an imposing farmhouse with three dormer windows. Proceed to climb out of this little valley, diagonally right (with vehicle tracks), crossing a stile *en route* to reach the top right-hand corner of the field, with a telegraph pole. Proceed onto the farm drive and turn left, following it down into the village of Ratley, with the village church clearly visible down to the left. Continue past the Rose and Crown, which dates back to 1098, and keep left in front of the church.

Beyond the church note the old post office on the left and continue to the Church Street sign. Here, the road curves round to the right but leave it here and go straight across the grass to a stone stile to the right of the manor farm drive gate.

Climb up, with the wall on your right, for 50m but leave it as it turns right. Carry straight on and down into a dip (slightly right) to a gate and stile. Proceed in the same direction, climbing steeply up the far side. As the ground levels, the route funnels into an old, rusty shed. Take the stile and then turn sharp right along a wide track with a tall hedge on the right, until the road is reached ❹. Turn right for 50m, (the tower of the Castle Inn is now in view again), then turn left just beyond 'Grange

Looking up from Radway to the tower on Edgehill

Hollow, at a stile and waymarker. Proceed narrowly, and in a raised position, via an oil storage tank, to the road. Cross diagonally left to the far side of the road to the Castle Inn, with its restored wooden walkway.

The inn, also known as the Round Tower, is thought to be based on Guy's Tower in Warwick Castle. It was built as a gatehouse for Radway Grange and became an inn in 1822. It is situated on the spot where Charles I raised his standard for the first major battle of the Civil War in 1642. Naturally the owners make good use of its history with a painting of the battle of Edgehill and other historical memorabilia in the lounge.

Descend the stone steps and concrete path with handrail to the right of the inn. Ignore a path off to the right and after 100m, take the stile straight ahead and leave the woods. Pause on the stone seat and note the obelisk in the trees over to the right. This glorious position gives fine views over to the village of Radway, with its church spire in the middle distance, and the site of the battle of 1642 (G.R.354493). Follow the fence and hedge on your right through two fields and down hill towards the village, along the edge of the Radway Grange estate. Take the stile in a wet corner, where the ground levels out and, quickly into a lane with a laurel hedge on the left.

Pass the duck pond on the right and Methodist chapel between the houses on the left.

The more impressive pond on the right at the west-end junction, belongs to the Grange. Turn right here, passing the lychgate to the rear of the church on your left and follow the road for a few hundred metres, via the swings, back to the centre of the village.

The plaque on the lychgate of Radway Church unusually recalls those who returned from the Great War, including Douglas Haig who was a regular visitor to the village. As Commander-in-Chief he planned the battle of the Somme in 1916 but suffered horrendous casualties. Passchendaele did nothing to re-establish his reputation the following year, but he enjoyed some successes towards the end of the war. After 1918 he gave his name to the British Legion Poppy Appeal. He died in 1928.

12

Tysoe and Epwell

Distance: 9 miles/14.5 km.
Features: Some superb views and charming villages. A marvellous
windmill overlooking a Jacobean Manor House at Compton
Wyniates.
Terrain: Moderate/strenuous. Hilly. Two climbs, mud after rain.
Maps: Landranger 151; Pathfinder 1021.
Car Parking: On the main road, near the Village Hall.
Public Transport: Limited services, Newmark Coaches
270/Stagecoach X70 (Stratford/Banbury).
Refreshments: Pubs in Epwell and Tysoe.
Start: Village Hall at Middle Tysoe (G.R. 341443).

This we consider to be a highlight of our collection.

Standing with your back to the Village Hall, turn left, and proceed
on the main road, quickly passing the Central Stores on your right
and the Fire Station on the left and follow this (on the right-hand
pavement) as it curves towards Upper Tysoe. Ahead, you will enjoy
glimpses of Windmill Hill, which is our first objective of the day.

At the top of the village, follow the main road as it curves sharp right
(Shipston Road) sign-posted to Brailes, Compton Wynyates and
Shipston. (As a point of reference, the Epwell Road joins here and is
where we re-emerge later on).

After about 100m on the left the windmill is just visible behind
'Touchstones' and here, for future reference, is the start of a public
footpath into Compton Wynyates Estate.

However, ignore this today and keep to the pavement on your right.
You will go past Meg Rivers' cake shop on your left. The road swings
left by the entrance to Tysoe Manor. Again, ignore the footpath signs
here and stay on the road out of the village. About 100m after leaving
the village the road bears sharply round to the right. As the bend
straightens out look for a gap and finger post on your left into a field.
Walk straight forward across the field (as waymarked) gradually
moving towards the left-hand hedge and meeting it at a field boundary.
Now continue upwards towards the windmill with the hedge on your
left. At the top of the second field go through a hedge gap in the
left-hand corner and continue with the hedge on your right.

Take your time at the top. This is one of the best vantage points in the
Midlands. Look back to the village of Tysoe with its church tower and,
over to the right to the wooded slopes of Edge Hill (site of the battle of
1642). The church spire at Radway, at the bottom of Edge Hill

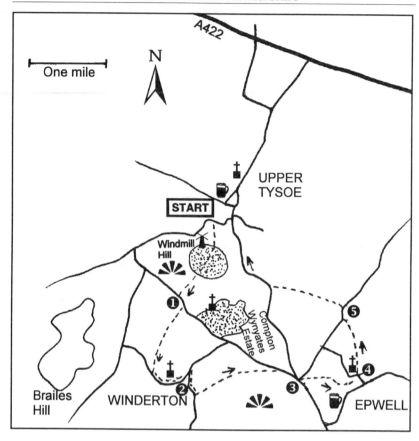

escarpment, is visible and beyond, on the same line are Burton Dassett Hills.

Follow the skyline round to your left and pick out Meon and Ilmington Hills (Ilmington with the two radio masts).

As we reluctantly leave the hilltop via a stile, on the same line the stunning Jacobean manor of Compton Wynyates in its own natural amphitheatre comes into view.

Cross the stile and turn sharp right and stay close to the wall for 100m until another stile and waymarker takes us left and downhill via some wooden steps. Ahead is the distinctive wooded top of Brailes Hill.

Pass a derelict barn on your left and cross a stile to join a track. Take another stile ahead (by a gate) and follow the track, and after another stile and gate join the pleasant green lane beyond to the road. ❶

At the road turn left, and after 150m, just beyond a semi-detached pair of houses on your right, take the waymark sign on your right into a field via a stile and proceed straight ahead to the next gate. Carry straight on to another gate in the same direction. At a stile you are joined by a hedge on your left and continue along the edge of two fields.

Our way is confirmed in the second field by a huge oak tree on our left with waymark signs.

Just beyond the oak leave the edge of the field at a corner and head forward in the general direction of a telegraph pole to a stile in the hedge beyond at a road.

At the road turn left and follow the road as it climbs gently into the village of Winderton with some impressive views of the church at Lower Brailes over to our right.

The view above Winderton

Follow the road sharply left past the church and on past some delightful properties and the telephone box to a T-junction. Turn right towards Brailes and note Qynton House (*no, this is not a misprint!*) on your left. Follow the road as it curves out of the village and note on the left the bungalow at Orchard View as a point of reference. Just beyond here the road turns round to the right. After 250m look for a waymarked gap and stile in the hedge on the left which is just before the road becomes tree-lined. ❷

Leave the road to cross the stile and pass between fences up to another stile after 50m. Continue on the same line with a wooden fence for company on your right. We gain height to enjoy extensive views around. Follow the fence into the corner and turn left along the hedge for about two-thirds of its length to a gap and stile on your right. Cross this and ignoring the gap on the left keep to the edge of the field with the hedge on your left. Very quickly a single large building appears below the radio mast.

At the next corner pause at a gap ahead. Our route is straight on across the field with the line generally towards the pylon on the ridge ahead. Depending on the time of year (and height of crop) it may be easier to turn right and then left in the corner around the edge of the field to arrive at the same stile on the right. Cross the little footbridge and then take a line diagonally left for 150m to a gap in the hedge, which is fairly obvious, before we start to climb.

At the stile in the gap take a line straight up the hill in the general direction of a telegraph pole and a large oak tree on the horizon. Pause at the top and look back – diagonally right of our line of ascent, on a good day, the distinctive lines of the Malvern Hills can be seen on the horizon. The view is simply stunning and you suddenly realise how high you have actually climbed. Cross the stile just to the right of the oak tree, in a corner.

The going is more level now as we follow the waymark signs around to the left to a gate and the entrance to an enclosed green lane. As the track turns sharp left to join the road, we carry straight on with a view of a thatched roof on our right. 'The Warren' is marked on the O.S. map. This bridleway takes us through a small plantation to the road. Turn right to the junction. ❸ At the junction turn right but, after only 10m, take the metal stile on your left and the diagonal path to the village of Epwell.

Continue on the same general line as you cross a fence stile to be joined by hawthorn trees and a barbed-wire fence on your left. The church tower comes into view. After 100m ignore the stile on the left and continue on the same line. (Epwell is a delightful village but much enjoyment can be lost with difficulties in finding the route beyond, therefore, sticking to our described route is well worthwhile). Pass through two fields, cross a stile and after a few metres turn left over an easily missed stile in a little clearing beside a telegraph pole. Take a line towards the church tower and houses to emerge at the road and turn right. Very quickly you arrive at the churchyard and the tempting sign on the right to the Chandlers Arms! If you take refreshments at the pub you will need to return to this signpost for our onward journey. ❹

For the pub follow the path which soon swings right to reach the road. The Chandlers Arms is now to the left.

Continuing from the signpost carry straight on past Church View and at the junction turn left.

Follow the road past 'Poppin' on the left and Broken Cartwheel on the right. About 100m past the Cartwheel, take the second footpath sign on the left to Rectory Farm (at Rectory Cottage).

Cross the cattle grid after only 50m or so and take a line diagonally left, away from the farm drive, towards the hedge and a stile, ignoring an earlier stile to the left. (Our stile is only 100m from the cattle grid and the farm drive is still only 50m to our right). Cross the footbridge and second stile. The farm drive is still reasonably close on the right as are the farm buildings. There is a distinctive round hill ahead. The farm drive beyond the buildings is new and we rejoin it at the cattle grid and gate. The route is indistinct but aim for an electricity pylon and rejoin the farm track.

Proceed to the road (Orchard Hill) ❺; turn right and after 100m turn left through the double gates at a signpost to Upper Tysoe 1¾ miles. Go across the first field, on an obvious track towards Downs Farm, until you reach a gap. Take a line which is diagonally right to a corner. (Depending on the time of year, easier going may be around the edge of the field to your right). In the corner there are two small gates. Take the left hand one. Cross the footbridge, turn sharp left, and then right at the corner following the edge of the field towards the farm. Keep the hedge on your left and ignore the gate and signs on your left.

Just as you approach the farm buildings, look across to your right and, in the far distance, the tower blocks of Coventry are visible. Take the gate into the farm itself and go straight on down the drive. As we approach the road our friendly windmill re-appears. At the road turn right and drop down into Upper Tysoe until reach the give way sign. Bear right here, back on familiar ground, and the short walk back to the start at Middle Tysoe.

13

Ilmington

Distance: 10 miles/16 km
Features: Fine ridge walking. Superb views. A splendid house and estate. Lovely unspoilt villages in a relatively unknown part of the Cotswolds.
Terrain: Strenuous with a number of steep climbs
Maps: Landranger 151; Pathfinder 1021/1020; Explorer 205.
Car Parking: Near the Howard Arms.
Public Transport: Guide Friday service 23 from Stratford-upon-Avon.
Refreshments: Pubs in Ilmington and Ebrington.
Start: Ilmington G.R. 214435

IT MAY be argued that this is one of the finest lowland walks in the United Kingdom. This bold claim is put into perspective at the end of a day full of delights and interest and which affords some breathtaking views. Enjoy.

The start of the walk is at the Howard Arms in Ilmington. Put on your boots at the bench with your back to the pub and then proceed right up the no-through road, passing the village stores on your right. The road quickly narrows into a delightful lane with a brook for company on your right. The cascade on the right is fed by the village pond which is worth exploring on another occasion. To your left you are given glimpses of the manor house gardens.

At the end of the lane, keep bearing round to the right, with the water on your right, until you quickly reach the back of the church. Turn left on the path and follow it around the churchyard, with the church itself on your right. Pause, for a moment, at the side entrance with the ancient tomb with iron railings dating back to the mid 1700s, and a variety of interesting masonry. Follow the limes until you reach the road opposite 'Church View by the notice board. Turn left, pass the old school house and, after 50m, turn right in front of M.D.Vincents (Hurdle-maker). After 50m, the made-up road ends but continue in the same direction, steeply up a sunken track, over-hung with large trees, to a gate.

Beyond the gate you emerge into a field. Proceed in the same direction keeping over to the hedge on the right. Ignore the stile and all the temptations of waymarkers off to the right, but continue in the same direction as the ground levels out. The views back across the village are already impressive with our favourite, Brailes Hill, over to the right with its wooded top and the Edge Hill escarpment forming the horizon beyond it. You can appreciate from here, the delightful location of

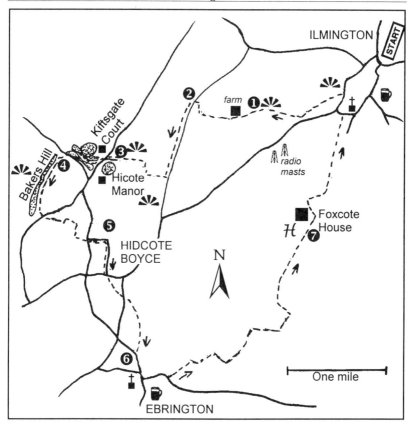

Ilmington. The hedge swings right as you reach a farm track with a tarmac road close by for reference, on the left.

Turn right onto the farm track, via a stile or a wicket gate, and follow it for 50m to a gate. Proceed straight on, enjoying views to the right and ahead towards Stratford. Pass a blue waymarker, go through a gate, then go left through another gate, ignoring the grassy track up to the farm.

Continue through two further gates, which are only 50m apart, on a track with wooden rails on both sides. The farm at Lark Stoke comes into view ❶ and our route takes a line to the left of this. Up on the left, the twin radio masts, which locate Ilmington for many miles around, are clearly visible. The path is well walked. Keep over to the left by the wooden rails and descend to another gate with stile and blue waymarker.

Beyond this, continue in the same direction, and the farm comes back into view. The area is spectacular and remote. Drop down steeply again before reaching the farm, keeping the pond on your right, to a gate and footbridge. Beyond the footbridge, go diagonally right, to a metal gate, cross the stream, and climb steeply up to the left, on a well-marked route.

As you draw level with the farm at the top of this steep section, don't be tempted off right towards it, but rather take the small metal gate straight ahead (with waymarker) into the woods. Carry on in the same direction on what can be a muddy path, until, shortly after the little footbridge with handrail, emerge on a wide track at right angles.

At this junction (there is a waymarker post) turn right, and proceed quickly to the edge of the woods where the track enters a field. Turn sharp left here and follow the edge of the field uphill. Keep the hedge on your left and aim for a single large tree on the skyline, where you emerge at a lane. ❷ Straight-ahead is Meon Hill, ancient hill fort and, supposedly, a site of witches.

Turn left and follow the lane uphill, with the twin radio masts increasingly prominent over to the left, and a second radio installation gradually coming into view ahead. Over to the far left horizon is the Edge Hill escarpment. As you approach the radio station on the right, a gap in the hedge on your right gives glimpses of the trig point which is marked on the map.

When you reach the radio station, a track crosses the lane at right angles. Turn right here, with a stone post on the left (and waymarker), and leave the radio station on your right. Straight ahead, Breedon Hill is visible and, just to the right, on a clear day, the distinctive outline of the Malvern Hills.

Follow the wide track as it swings right and then left and then descends towards Hidcote Gardens with a line of Scots pines diagonally over to the right in the middle distance. The roof of Hidcote House quickly comes into view and our route takes us straight on, between the car parks (to the left and right), and down the main drive which is wooded and lined on the right with low posts. The house and garden are well worth a visit on another occasion.

Continue to the end of the drive to the junction where Mickleton is left and Stratford is signed right. ❸ Pause at the wall just behind this signpost and look down the valley that is our onward route.

Take the large blue wooden gate on your right and then turn sharp left and proceed down the middle of the valley, passing a large cedar tree on your left. This is a lovely spot.

Proceed through the muddy gateway at the bottom of the hill, where the wooden railings funnel in from right and left. Beyond the gateway keep over to the left and follow the wooden fence on the edge of the woods (with waymarkers). Look up to the right and glimpse the house at Kiftsgate Court, above the gorse, with a magnificent magnolia in the spring. There are an infinite variety of trees on the estate to enjoy from our path.

After 300m, the wooden fence turns sharp left at a willow tree. Cross the stream here and turn sharp right on the far bank and follow it for 30m. Straight ahead, is a single magnificent cedar tree. Our line is, however, well to the left of this, climbing diagonally left to the far end of the woods up on our left (with three Scots pines).

At this corner, Mickleton is now visible with its church spire (the large cedar tree is 100m to our right). Follow the fence sharp left and uphill, initially rather unpromisingly, to a gate with a metal footpath sign. (From the corner, don't be tempted straight on towards a metal gate in the hedge 100m ahead).

Cross the road and climb the muddy steps through the trees, to emerge on the edge of a field via a stile – Heart of England Way. ❹ Turn right and follow the edge of the field with the woods on the right. After 200m, the path takes us into the woods again, in a raised position known as Bakers Hill. The path is obvious with huge beech trees and spectacular views to enjoy.

Emerge from the trees and follow the edge of the field, with the hedge on your left, for 200m until you reach a track just in front of a low shed and barn. Turn left here for just 10m to a junction with a tiny green triangle. Cross diagonally left over this track into another field, and follow its edge with the hedge on your left, towards Hidcote Boyce.

In the far corner of the field the path drops down to a little footbridge. Cross it, turn sharp left, and continue to follow the edge of the field with a brook on your left. Follow the path as it swings left, then right, for 150m where there is a waymarker post, and a hedge comes in from the right. Turn 90 degrees right here to follow the hedge on your left across the field.

After 200m turn left at the gate and stile with a waymarker. Proceed up the double track, which is lined with hedges on both sides, to a gate at the road. ❺ Cross straight over and proceed up the road into Hidcote Boyce – a typical, unspoilt Cotswold village.

Pass the village phone box and notice board on your right and, after another 50m, follow the road round to the right, ignoring the road straight ahead which leads to Top Farm.

Follow the road out of the village. The first junction is a right-hand turn to Ebrington. Leave the road here at a gate, stile, and footpath sign, which is diagonally right across the junction. In the field a track appears to take us down slightly right – ignore this and keep at the same height across the field, bearing slightly left if anything. The path is not obvious here. Broadway Tower is visible here on the right-hand horizon. A large 'aircraft hanger' of a barn comes into view. Don't be drawn down to this. Our route is across the field, 200m up to the left of the barn, between two willows at a water trough and stile.

Bear slightly left across the next field, again looking for a waymarker between two willows. The roofs of Ebrington come into view ahead. Take the stile and carry on in the same direction, to a waymarker and stile. Take a line slightly left for 100m, up to a stile in the hedge, to re-emerge at the road. Turn right for 30m and then, at the sign, leave the road on the left via a stile.

Carry on diagonally right to a waymarker post. Cross the stile and carry on beneath the telegraph wires in the same direction. Cross a stile about 50m to the right of the far right corner of the field. Go over a footbridge and continue forward with a hedge on your left. Almost at the end of the field bear very slightly left along a farm track, passing a soccer field on the left, to emerge at the road by the playing fields sign. Turn left. Continue past the village hall on your right – make a contribution if you wish!

At the give-way sign, carry straight on in the same direction, passing the school on your left, as the Ebrington Arms comes into view.

Take a break on the metal seats around the trees in front of the pub and Victoria Terrace. ❻

The way continues in the same direction, leaving the little village green on your right. (If leaving the pub, remember to turn right at the road!)

Continue past the phone box on the right and, in turn, the restored village spring on the left. When the houses end the road swings round to the right. There is also a no-through road off to the left here. We, however, carry straight on between the two, on a metalled track with a footpath sign.

Continue to follow the track and, leaving a farm house over to your left, bear right at the junction (left, taking you to the house). Look carefully to the field to the right of the house and spot the sculptures of various figures (visible at the time of writing).

A raised fuel tank comes into view and after about 150m turn left in front of it at the waymarker post. Meanwhile, over to our left now is a line of poplars and, directly behind them, a line of conifers. 400m on, beyond the fuel tank, the double track emerges/stops at the edge of a field at a spot with various items of equipment, building materials, and bits and pieces.

There is a waymarker post on the right and we turn sharp right here and proceed across the middle of the field on a well-worn path, dropping down to the hedge line at the bottom, to another waymarker post. The trees at the bottom screen a brook. Turn left and follow its edge generally towards the farm buildings.

Ignore the first gap on the right and continue for a total of 100m along the stream to a waymarker post. Turn right across the stream via the footbridge. Continue up the edge of the field, with the hedge on your right, for 100m to reach the farm track where you turn left towards the buildings. The two radio masts above Ilmington come back into view giving us the real impression that we are heading for home.

Proceed through the yard and, at the last building (with semi-circular roof), bear to the right, leaving it on your left. We are joined on the right by a coniferous wood.

As the edge of the wood swings right turn left at a junction of tracks. Follow the track, with a steep bank down to the left, until until you reach the gate in front of the lake beneath Foxcote House – a place of delightful tranquillity. Pause and enjoy. **❼**

Foxcote House

Climb away diagonally right, and in the same general direction, for 100m to a gate and enter the woods on a wide track with a large laurel just to the left and a tall wire fence on the right. 100m into the conifers the track swings round to the left. Fork right here (waymarkers) through the trees. We are simply avoiding the buildings on the left in the clearing.

Proceed through the trees (with arrows). After 100m you arrive at a track junction. Turn left here as indicated by the bridle way sign. Drop down into the dip and then steeply up the other side to join the main tarmac drive that serves the house. Turn right on the drive and leave the house behind you.

Look up diagonally left to spot a single building with black archway and three stone globes. Cross a cattle-grid and as you proceed along the drive note the line of trees on the ridge ahead. At the left hand end of the trees is a double gate that is our objective.

When you have drawn level with the single posh building (a barn) that we mentioned up on the left, look for a sign to leave the tarmac drive on your left, and follow the path up to the ridge with the hedge on your right.

On the ridge, our final high point, the views unfold again. This descent is particularly delightful on a summer's evening.

Cross straight over the track at the top and proceed downhill with the hedge on the right, towards the village of Ilmington.

Carry on down, via a number of stiles, in the same direction. As the ground levels out, the hedge becomes a series of willow trees. Don't be tempted off right through the trees, but carry on a further 50m and cross the stream by a single plank footbridge with handrail.

Turn left on the far side and proceed for another 100m and cross the stile. Pass along the end of the garden with silver birches and a wooden rail on your right. At the little junction of tracks, on the far side of the garden, turn left just in front of the telegraph pole. Don't be tempted with the waymarkers straight on. Proceed, to climb narrowly, and then emerge at the road opposite a cottage dated 1858.

Turn right downhill and, after 100m, take the left-hand turn to Admington and Mickleton. The church comes back into view and we are back on familiar ground. Pass the hurdle-maker on the left, schoolhouse on the right, and turn back into the churchyard by the notice board. (At the back of the church remember to turn right on the narrow path where the waymarkers urge you to go straight on). Re-trace your footsteps back to the Howard Arms at the end of what we hope has been a truly memorable day that finishes in tranquillity.

Radio masts on Ilmington Hill

14

Honington and Idlicote

> **Distance:** 5 miles/8 km.
> **Features:** The impressive estate village of Honington. There are superb views from Idlicote Hill.
> **Terrain:** One climb, moderate/easy.
> **Maps:** Landranger 151; Pathfinder 1021; Explorer 205.
> **Car Parking:** In the main village street.
> **Public Transport:** Nothing suitable.
> **Refreshments:** Take your own!
> **Start:** Honington village (near Shipston-on-Stour) G.R.264425.

THE start of the walk is at the lower end of the main village street at the private entrance to the Hall drive, marked by white gates and four pillars topped by more recent globes. With your back to these, turn left up the hill, through the village. Pass the P.O. box and telephone. The first right-hand turn is to Barcheston and Willington, with an old 'Best Kept Village sign. Opposite this, on the left, is a waymark post and waymarker, taking us past Victoria Cottage and, briefly, across the end of the garden, all of which is well waymarked.

Take a stile into a field and make straight across to another stile and waymarker in the conifers ahead. Over to the left are the grounds of the estate at Honington Hall. 20m through the conifers take an older stile and turn right, through an area, screened from a garden, to the road where you turn left. ❶

Proceed to the end of the cottages on the right (100m), and look for a waymark post into a field on the right by a brook. Enter the field and

The entrance gates to Honington Hall

73

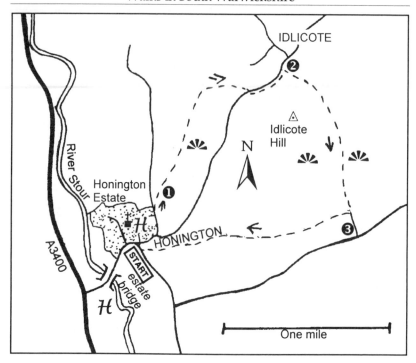

follow the fence on your left, parallel to the road, for about 200m until you reach a gate, (the gate is only about 30m from the road). The views over to the left are of the impressive frontage to Honington Hall and, further right, the spire of the church at Tredington (a village not blessed with many footpaths but well worth a visit all the same).

From the gate take a line diagonally right, up hill, and aim for a point at the top right-hand end of the trees in front. A pair of wooden gates come into view, just in front of a large mass of brambles, and give access to the next field. The area is not particularly well walked or waymarked beyond the wooden gates. Follow the trees and tall hedge on your left until it ends suddenly at a gap about 30m before the far side of the field. Look left and be re-assured by the direct line between this point, the Dutch barn in the valley, and the church spire beyond. Carry straight on at the gap to a corner and then follow the edge of the field round to the right. After 50m, continue to follow the edge as it turns left (with a large ditch on the left).

Follow the edge of the field right once again as you draw level with Granby Hill Farm, and then follow the hedge on your left, until you reach the road. At the road turn left and, after 100m, note the entrance to Whitehouse Farm on the left (our path is marked emerging here, on the map). After about 200m look out for a gap on the left (from where there is a good view of Idlicote House). The path should apparently run through this gap and then diagonally right to reach the road beside the entrance drive to Whitehouse Farm. However, although the far end is waymarked, there were, at the time of writing, no signs of access here and we had to continue straight on (along a clearly used path) to the road where we turned left for 100m to meet the Whitehouse Farm drive. Look out to see if the right of way has been opened up.

Carry straight on past this drive and follow the road as three single-storey gate houses come into view at the drive entrance to the estate house at Idlicote (with pillars and globes). Carry straight on past these, as the road rises ahead. Almost at the brow of the hill, look for a red brick walled garden on the left and, opposite here, take the stile on the right, with public footpath sign, to leave the road at right-angles and climb the hill. ❷ As you reach the high point, the village of Whatcote is visible, with its church tower, over to the left, as is Oxhill Hill just left and beyond. Continue in the same direction, with an interesting circular copse on your left. Don't be drawn off line by tempting gates and little footbridges to the right.

Follow the hedge on the right on a wide grassy track, climbing gradually to a line of trees. Note the wind pump over to the right.

Almost at the high point, look over to the right, to the spire at Tredington church. Continue to cross a farm drive, in a delightful, raised position and carry on to a line of trees. Some lovely views unfold ahead. Take the grassy spur across the middle of the field, giving a real sense of a raised plateau. At the highest point look across left to get a good view of the Tysoe windmill.

Drop down the far side towards a white cottage at the right-hand end of a line of poplars. Just before the tarmac drive, turn right, leaving the white cottage close by, on the left. ❸ Follow the edge of the field with the hedge on the left. The going is level and obvious. Pause and look back, over your right shoulder, to our descent of a few minutes ago and to the four trees on the horizon. At the end of the field, cross the brook at a gap and then proceed diagonally left across another field for 100m, to a gap in the hedge. The gap is deeper on arrival.

Proceed through the small, wooden gate and continue across the field in the same direction. Go through a double metal gate on the far

The village green, Honington

side as we are joined by a thorn hedge on the left. Behind is another good view of the windmill. We are re-assured by the metal frame of an old barn coming into view. Go straight on past this (the hedge ends on the left), and proceed for another 200m to more metal gates with a wooden gate on their left. Immediately past these it is worth pausing at the metal gate on the left, for a view of Shipston down to our right. It is also possible to pick out the slanting tower of the church at Barcheston straight ahead in the middle distance.

Continue forward along a wide grassy track that is, in places, just below the level of the field to the right as it climbs slightly to a final rise.

The village of Honington comes back into view, as does the church spire at Tredington. As you approach the village pass through two wicket gates, then take a gate into the road and turn right. After 100m, we are back on familiar ground at a T-junction. Turn left and retrace your steps back through the village.

15

Sutton-under-Brailes

Distance: 6 miles/9.5 km.
Features: A majestic hill. Lovely unspoilt villages in a relatively little known area. Some fine views.
Terrain: One steep climb. Moderate.
Maps: Landranger 151; Pathfinder 1021/1044.
Car Parking: Village centre, Sutton-under-Brailes.
Public Transport: Guide Friday service 23 from Stratford-upon-Avon. Alight in Upper Brailes at the Gate Inn. With your back to the inn turn left and walk for about 50m where there is a kissing gate on the left. Now start reading from ★ on p. 79.
Refreshments: Pubs in Lower Brailes and Upper Brailes.
Start: Sutton-under-Brailes village (G.R.301374).

START by the impressive, ancient, hollow oak stump in the centre of the village of Sutton-under-Brailes, with a convenient bench, just to one side, for putting on boots. With your back to the notice board (just behind the old tree), proceed straight ahead down the road which forms the T-junction, to Stourton and Long Compton. After 50m, leave the road and enter a narrow lane on the left. (There is an old, wooden footpath sign and a waymark in the hedge on the left). Proceed between the cottage (left) and wooden garage (on the right). Follow the lane which is lined by tall hedges, for 100m, until it ends. Take the stile on the left, with waymarker, and proceed at right angles to the lane across the field.

After 100m, take the stile and waymarker in the general direction of the church tower which is on our onward journey. Cross the stile and then proceed for 40m to another in a slight dip. Beyond this little stone bridge and stile, head diagonally right towards the willows. Cross the stream, via the concrete footbridge in the trees, and proceed for a further 40m to cross another footbridge and a stile. The going is pretty obvious. Follow the edge of the field for 20m and then turn left through the tall hedge over a stile and yet another footbridge.

Cross straight over the lane to enter Brailes Golf Club, via stile and footbridge. (*Beware golf balls – which may also come from the left!*). Proceed straight on to pick up a waymark post. The route is pretty obvious and well waymarked and follows the top of a slight rise with a stream down to the left. A line of red stakes takes us into the general area of the club house, which we pass over to our left, and then beyond it on a gravel track.

Follow this track round to the green machinery hut with corrugated roof, and then between two large trees with waymarker. If you look

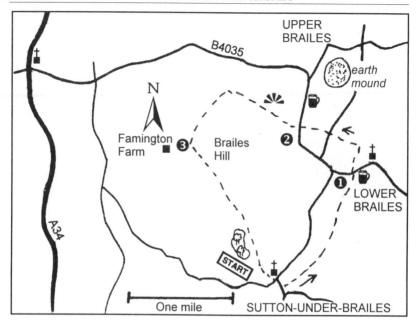

right to the ridge here you will see a radio mast. Descend the steps and cross the footbridge. Eventually leave the golf course at a stile next to a pair of metal gates. The church tower at Brailes is now clearly in view and we follow the obvious route along the edge of the field. After crossing two stiles we are joined by a farm track from the right.

Leave the farm drive again, quickly, before it crosses the stream, to head, with a hedge on the left, once again for the church. Just after swinging right at the end of the field cross a stile into a second field. Continue with a hedge on the left through two more fields until a waymarker and stile leads onto a lane.

Cross straight over the lane and straight on through the wooden gate. After 100m, take the right fork at a wall. Follow the wall on your left (ignore the stile on the right), and follow it to the road at a double fronted white house. ❶ Turn left for 20m and then, at the archway of the George Hotel cross over the road and proceed up Butchers Lane. Pass Feldon House, with the church close by on the right and the spire at Winderton coming into view straight ahead.

Continue up the new tarmac drive towards Glebe Farm and, before you reach the farm and as you think you are off route on a private drive, take the stile on the left. (There is a gate on your right into the cemetery as a point of reference). The church itself is well worth a look.

Proceed straight across the field, making for the right-hand end of a line of tall trees. On the far side of the field we are re-assured by a waymark post. Drop down over a bridge and cross the little meadow, with trees to your left, and ascend the steps on the far side.

The western flank of Brailes Hill

At the top, continue in the same direction, keeping the wire fence on your right. After 100m, cross the stile and carry on in the same direction crossing some pronounced ridge and furrow, towards a gate. Diagonally left, we start to view Brailes Hill with its distinctive clump of trees. Over to the right on the gorse covered hill there is evidence of an ancient earthworks. Take the stile to the right of the gate, with an old tree trunk to the left for reference.

Proceed along the well walked path, across the middle of the next field. Don't be tempted off to the earthworks but continue in the same direction.

Cross straight over the road, and enter the next field, via a stile. Continue in the same direction. As the single-story building, with the clock tower, comes into view, cross the brook. Keep tight over to the right-hand hedge and leave the clock tower on your left. A kissing gate gives access to the road.

★ *Bus travellers start here.*

❷ Cross straight over (50m to the right is the Gate Inn), and proceed up Gilletts Lane, passing Hill-Side House. At the top of the lane a wooden five bar gate gives access to Honeysuckle Cottage. Proceed straight on to the left of the cottage and on through the small white gate.

Continue to climb diagonally right, with trees and bushes on the left and a double telegraph pole about 20m to the right, heading up to a single large tree. Just behind it is another stile and waymarker for re-assurance. Already we have gained sufficient height at this stile to enjoy marvellous views back over our earlier route.

Climb steeply beyond the stile, in an enclosed gully, to emerge at a large chestnut tree as the ground levels out. We are given glimpses, over to the left, of the trees at the top of Brailes Hill that are now much closer. There is also a single building just to their left with a steep pitched roof.

Proceed about 200m beyond the tree to another stile, across scrub-land (marked as route58). Pause again to look back towards Upper and Lower Brailes and the spire of Winderton church in a delightful position over to your left and, beyond it and left the tree covered slopes of Edge Hill.

Over the stile continue forward on level going, with the high point now closer at hand on the left. On the far side of this large, flat field, we descend steeply through the trees with, again, magnificent views straight ahead.

At the bottom of the slope you emerge from the trees and go diagonally left, as indicated by the waymarker post, across the field. Straight ahead are the twin radio masts on Ilmington Hill. After 100m, you pass beneath the telegraph wires and continue for a further 30m. Turn left at a vague junction (the path does continue ahead), and contour around the hill. Don't lose any more height. We find ourselves close to the gorse again and soon we join a farm track (rough going), and opposite a metal gate turn right (blue waymarker). Left is a private drive.

Follow the track for 200m to a T-junction where we turn left through a gate marked by a blue waymarker. Climb briefly and continue to contour on a wide track. Eventually our way is barred by a 'Private, Keep Out' sign and metal gate. Leave the track to the right, via a wooden gate. Proceed along the edge of the field in the same general direction, dropping down slightly to the left.

We are re-assured by a waymarker (57a) on a large tree, where we leave the broad track. The area is well walked and ridden and follows an obvious line down to the farm buildings. A small, circular copse is evident over to our right in the field. There appears to be a Scots pine growing out of the roof of the farm ahead (Famington Farm).

At the bottom of the long descent you arrive at a hedge where you turn left (waymark post). Follow the hedge on your right. The farm is now obviously derelict. Another red brick farm comes into view straight ahead and we need to be looking for a left-hand turn to leave the track in about 300m Our route goes through a gap in the hedge. A further 100m, beyond this gap, a barrel-top barn comes into view to the right of the red brick farmhouse and we arrive at two waymarkers marking a crossing path. Our route is off to the left, leaving the track. (For reference, after 30m, a right-hand turn here would take us to a small wooden footbridge). ❸

Proceed diagonally right (S.E.) across the large field up again, towards the line of trees at the bottom of the hill. On the far side of the field we pass a single tree about 30m over to our left, as a point of reference. A little bridge leads to a stile. Turn right and then, after only 10m, swing round to the left (no.68) to climb steeply up through the gorse (waymarker on tree) – the yellow gorse combining delightfully with bluebells in late April/early May.

As you approach the top the way narrows between the bushes to reach a metal gate and stile (avoid swinging off to the right) This last climb of the day is well worth the effort and we are quickly rewarded with magnificent views. Beyond the stile, turn sharp left and continue to climb gently. The metal fence is, initially, only 10m to our left but our line is straight on as the fence curves away to the left.

After about 100m, the ground levels out and our way swings round to the right and we are joined by another fence on the left (and waymarker). We find ourselves in a little corridor between this fence and the hawthorn bushes at the top of the slope to our right. Very quickly a metal gate comes into view with a waymarker on its left-hand upright. Beyond this gate the going is more even and we stay close to the hedge on the left. Ignore the gate on the left (no.61), with blue waymarker, and continue in the same direction, passing a little group of small Scots pines on your left (for reference).

We now begin our descent back to the village where we started. If you glance over diagonally left to the ridge, you will see the radio mast, which was our companion on the outward journey. The track soon becomes a double track and the stunted church tower in the village (which we pass next to) comes into view. Go straight through the metal gate, whose uprights are metal-capped. Pause for a last look at the view. Just ahead, to the right, is a nice stand of mixed woodland with pine and poplars, and our way down to this is obvious.

Go straight through the gate as you draw level with these private woods, and enjoy the hidden pool to the right. Proceed down the made-up drive. Just when you think you have reached home we are diverted off the drive to the left, at a waymarker and stile. This is just before the private drive and 'Keep Out' sign. Follow the path across the field towards the church, which is now close at hand.

Take the stile into the orchard and proceed in the same direction, looking for a gate by the telegraph pole to the right of the church. Take the two stiles, which are close together, to emerge onto the lane. (The big wooden 'wheels' on the cottage on the left must be remnants of the old belfry). Turn left and follow the road round into the centre of the village.

Bus travellers now continue reading from the start on page 77.

16

Shipston and Great Wolford

Distance: 12½ miles/20 km.
Features: A walk dominated by church towers and spires. Lovely distant views and some interesting villages *en route*.
Maps: Landranger 151; Pathfinder 1021/1044.
Car Parking: Car park opposite the Old Mill Hotel, Shipston-on-Stour.
Public Transport: Stagecoach bus service X50 (Stratford-upon-Avon/Oxford).
Refreshments: Pubs in Shipston, Great Wolford and Todenham.
Start: The bridge car park, Shipston-on-Stour, opposite the Old Mill Hotel on the Brailles Road (G.R.261405), which is left off the main road from Stratford.

TURN left out of the car park over the river bridge and continue past the left turn to Honington for 20m and then take the stile and waymark sign off to the right (this is well marked). Initially with a row of trees on the right our route to the little hamlet of Barcheston is obvious, following the River Stour which keeps us company over to our right. As the church tower of St. Martins comes into view follow the telegraph poles (over your right), towards the village. The village church appears to be in a hollow and the 'leaning tower' rather out of proportion to the body of the church.

Just beyond a line level with the church, take the stile in the corner by a wall. Emerge onto a lane and turn left. Walk past the manor house

Barcheston Church

82

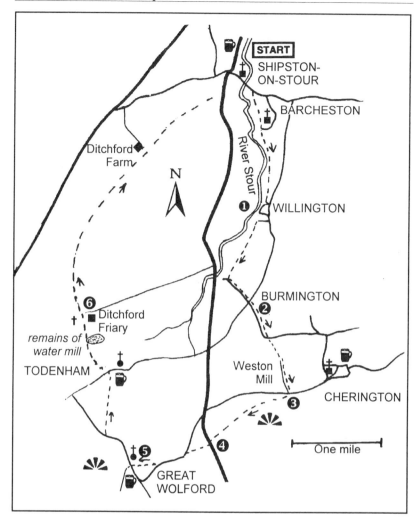

and, after 50m or so, the road swings sharp round to the left (level with the church gate) where there is an old pump on your left – take a quick look! At this corner turn right (with waymark sign) into the field towards the village of Willington.

The path takes a direct line across the field. Brailes Hill, our regular companion today, is visible on the left with its isolated wooded top.

On the far side of the field cross a stile and carry on in the same direction (although there is a large collection of various signs). The hamlet of Willington comes into view. Eventually, after two more fields, an orange gate close to the river gives access to a narrow lane beside two bridges. Don't cross these but rather carry on forward up the surfaced path into the village. 100m after the bridges you arrive at the road where you turn right.

Walk past the cricket fanatics at 'Mid-wicket' and, opposite, notice the penny-farthing above the door at 'Brook Cottages'.

Just beyond these two houses the road bends sharp round to the left. Go straight on here, leaving the road by Rushway House and the post box. Cross the stream via a footbridge (with bent handrail) and climb gently up to Manor Farm with the old farm house on your right and the 'mushroom' lined drive off left. Carry straight on in the same direction and take the stile on the left opposite the old brick barn with stone stairs.

After a further 50m take another stile into a field, continuing forward with a fence on the right. Admire the large house to the right with the walled garden and, over to its left, a chapel that is marked on the O.S. map. This is Tidmington. ❶

Take the stile into a narrow field that, after only 50m, takes you to a footbridge. Cross the bridge and continue in the same direction (with waymark sign). Note the ridge and furrow in this field, (which changes direction over to your right). As we cross the field our way tends over towards the far left-hand corner and a stile. Follow the edge of the next field to the road and the village of Burmington. Turn left along the road and note the village church of St. Nicholas and St. Barnabas.

Proceed uphill through the village passing the restored, raised storage barn, which is almost alpine in appearance. At the crossroads at the top of the village, cross straight over onto the Cherington Road. The road climbs quite steeply into a lovely elevated position with the church spire at Todenham visible over to our right on the return journey. ❷

At the brow of the hill the ground levels out and swings left. 150m beyond the left-hand bend, as a large new dwelling appears over to the left (hedges may obscure your view of this), look for double metal gates and waymarker on the right. Turn right here and descend a rather unusual beautiful avenue of oaks towards Weston Mill. As the ground levels out at the bottom, look for a gate and waymarker on the left next to a large meander in the stream. Take the gate and, after 100m, another, as the track leads towards the farm buildings, crossing the stream. Proceed through the farm yard and turn right onto the drive (ignore the waymarked route straight ahead) and follow it until you reach the road. ❸

Cross straight over and take the gate immediately on your right at a public bridleway sign (there is a Dutch barn up to the right for reference). Our route, however, is well to the right of the barn, to the right-hand end of the line of trees. Take the small gate onto the track and then the next gate straight ahead with waymark sign, ignore the drive to the left. Continue on the edge of the field with the woodland on your left. Look over to the right and pick out the double line of trees that was our descent earlier.

Keep close over to the left. Go through a gate, still keeping the trees on your left. At a small gap where the ground falls away, make straight down to the footbridge in the valley, leaving the edge of the woods. A delightful piece of water comes into view with an island. Buzzards have been seen in this area. Cross the wooden footbridge with waymarker and continue in the same direction as our way climbs steadily with a hedge on our left.

As you reach the corner of the field and the ground levels out, pause and look back. Carry straight on, leaving the field with large beech trees to your right and a waymark post for reassurance. Swing slightly right and, with a tall hedge on your left, descend the next field to the road. ❹ Turn left opposite 'Double Lodges'. After 50m, take the gate with waymark sign on the right. Proceed quickly to another gate and, beyond this, take a line diagonally left across the next field up towards the Dutch barn at the end of a line of trees.

At the barn, proceed through a series of gates (with the barn on your left) in, generally, the same direction but rather than continuing down the muddy farm drive take the small gate to the right which gives access to a field. The church spire at Great Wolford is directly ahead and is *en route*. Take a line just to the right of the cottage in the field and through a gate onto the road. Turn left, cross over and follow the pavement downhill towards the village.

Cross the restored Nethercote Bridge and, after a further 100m, opposite 'Nethercote Arches', take the right-hand turn with gate and waymark post on the well walked path up to the church. Keep the church on your left and carry on down to the junction by the phone box. ❺ Our route is right here but the excellent Fox and Hounds is 150m straight ahead (closed Sunday nights and all day Monday)! However, turn right (or left if it is after the pub!) towards the village of Todenham. Follow the road as it swings left and down out of the village as the church spire comes into view over to the right.

Cross the stream at the bottom by Brook Cottages and continue past the entrance to Mount Sorrell. 300m beyond this farm entrance, before the road starts to rise, look for the footpath post off to the right through a gap in the hedge Take a direct line to the spire. After 100m, cross a

The skyline of Great Wolford

85

The village pub and church at Todenham

small wooden footbridge at the end of a line of willows and proceed for another 50m across a narrow field to a stile.

Continue with the hedge on your right and, soon, a split-level barn comes into view. Aim for the left-hand end of the building, crossing a stile *en route*. Go through the gate and continue on the same line, to a gap in the hedge ahead. Go through the gap (there is no stile at the time of writing), and cut down, diagonally right, to a gate which leads onto a drive that takes you up into the village (sub-station on the right for reference).

At the main road turn left. The building on your right is the Farmers Arms pub (with silver extractor vent). 150m beyond the pub you come to the old school house on your right (now the village hall), with a bell on the roof. Just before this take the path on your right, passing Ash House. Pass the tennis court and Dutch barn on your right and, at the gate, carry straight on through the gate and look for a large building in the valley with a white gable end facing you. This is Ditchford Friary. Our general line is just to the left of this. Ahead, on the ridge, you can see the familiar Ilmington Hill.

From the gate go straight across the field, tending slightly right, to drop down onto a track along which you turn left, with a hedge on your right, to a gate (this is only 200m from the first gate). Pass a little dew-pond on the left and carry straight on through the gate. Continue between hedges on a wide track. Note the equestrian activity on your left. A large lake with an island becomes evident in the middle distance. This is a well-used bridleway. As we emerge into a field a single, derelict brick building comes into view and our line is just to the right of this (the main track curves away to the right). Just before the footbridge, the overgrown remains of an old mill are of interest. Cross the brook and continue, via two gates, then soon over a bridge and waymarked gate by the side of a pool, and around the edge of an enclosure, to reach via a gate the drive just to the left of Ditchford Friary. **❻**

Ignore the stile straight over the road but, rather, turn right and walk past the impressive front of the Friary. On a recent visit there were peacocks, peahens and their chicks (peachicks?) in an enclosure beside the path. As you arrive at the green barn just beyond it, turn left and take the obvious track across the field, crossing a cattle grid after about 40m. The track climbs quite steeply and affords splendid views back to the south and west. As you reach the brow of the hill and begin to descend, a windpump appears diagonally left.

At the junction of the tracks turn right towards the house with the conservatory. Before you reach the house however, the route divides and our route is off to the right as indicated by the blue way-marker. Our friendly group of trees on top of Brailes Hill is, again, clearly visible ahead. Ignore the first left turn which takes you back to Ditchford Farm, and carry straight on along a now grassy track. Our way continues, very obviously, between hedges soon passing a narrow strip of woodland on the right. About 300m beyond the woodland go through a gate, then after another few metres turn left through a waymarked wooden gate and walk with a hedge on the right to reach Pig Brook.

Cross the wooden footbridge over the brook. The line takes us over the middle of the next field, on a well-walked path, to a hedge end. Carry on the same line, keeping the hedge on your left. After 150m cross a little wooden footbridge.

We are now starting our last ascent that will give us a view over Shipston and our starting point. Our route now becomes more enclosed with trees and brambles on both sides. We start to climb more steeply and the seat on the left at the top is most welcome. This sting in the tail is well worth it, as the roof tops of the town now come into view and we drop down a wide grassy lane with hedges on both sides.

Go through a gate as you reach the houses onto a tarmac path. When you reach the road turn right and follow it into the town centre, passing the vets on your left. At a T-junction you will see the black and white Horseshoe pub straight ahead. Cross to it and turn right (left for the bus stop) and follow the pavement round to the left onto the B4035 towards Brailes and the car park is on the left.

17

Blockley and Longborough

Distance: 10½ miles/17 km.
Features: A walk packed with variety and interest. The lovely Cotswold villages of Blockley and Bourton-on-the-Hill. The delightful, remote Hinchwick valley, one of the hidden gems of the North Cotswolds. Fine views. The picturesque Sezincote Estate.
Terrain: Several climbs. Moderate – strenuous.
Maps: Landranger 151/163; Pathfinder 1043/1044.
Car Parking: Around the Village Green, near the post office.
Public Transport: Nothing suitable.
Refreshments: Pubs in Blockley, Longborough and Bourton-on-the-Hill.
Start: Blockley Post Office Stores.(G.R.164349).

W ITH your back to the Post Office Stores, facing the bowling green, turn right and follow the road up Bell Lane as it climbs slightly and then swings round to the right (Heart of England Way sign), and proceed past the Crown Hotel on your right.

We are joined on the right by a large wall which contains (at ground level) Russells Spring. Continue past Days Lane on your right and, as we begin to leave the village, look for the next right, that is a private road and is marked by a post box and public footpath sign. This is opposite a property known as Rosedale on the left. Turn right here and, after 100m, cross the cattle grid and keep left at the fork, towards the Northwick Estate. Follow the wide, obvious track through the trees and onward to a building in open country on your right. A glance back will already show how far we have climbed with impressive views beyond the village. At the cottage and barn on the right (Warren Farm) carry straight on up in the same direction (don't be tempted by the track that joins from the left).

Where the track turns sharp right at a gap in the hedge, leave it and carry straight on across the field on an obvious track towards the line of trees. Look back for the last time and go through the gate to the road. ❶ Turn right but, after only 20m, turn left at a footpath sign and stile into a field. Stay close to the broken stone wall on the right. When the wall ends follow the wire fence on what becomes a wide sunken track that descends to some mixed woodland.

At the bottom of the hill, in a typical unspoilt hollow with the farm complex of Far Upton Wold, are two gates that are 50m apart. Beyond the second gate, do not be drawn off right towards the house but stay left, going between the three trees straight ahead and the stone wall to the left. We are quickly re-assured by a gate in the left-hand corner and

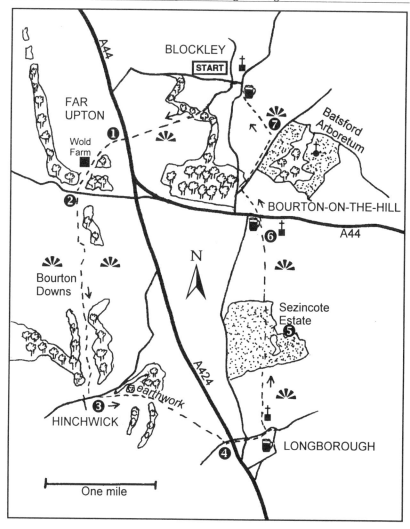

waymarker. Beyond the gate stay close to the metal fence on the right. After 100m, cross the stream and leave the fence to carry on down towards the cottages and the drive. The tranquillity is only interrupted by the noise from the rookery.

Cross the cattle grid and proceed down the drive, between the buildings, to the road ❷, with a pond on the right at the junction. Bear very slightly left and then cross straight over to go through the metal gate with metal bridge and way sign

Don't be drawn off left towards the valley but, rather, stay close over to the fence and bushes on the right, and climb quite steeply up what can be a muddy track. At the top of the rise there are two gates on your right. Take the left-hand metal one of these, with waymarker. Keep over to the left and spot another waymarker about 50m ahead.

Proceed through the trees, keeping to the left, to another blue waymarker after 50m, passing a single, large tree (with S.L.R. inscribed) on your left. Continue to follow the left-hand hedge until, about 100m before the fence and gate at the end of the field, a finger post directs you away diagonally right to climb to a gate at the top of the field. Go through the small wooden gate (with large chain and counter-balance) in the top corner with a waymarker, and stay close to the hedge on the right.

A line of conifers comes into view ahead and these are en route. Leave the field by a small, wooden gate in the wall at the far end by the telegraph pole. Turn left and then, after 75m on a wide track, turn right just in front of the line of conifers. Just beyond the end of these there is an ancient stone post, as a point of reference, and a waymarker.

We can now enjoy level walking on a wide track above the Hinchwick Valley, with extensive views over the Bourton Downs to our right. After 400m the track makes a right-angled turn towards a barn. Follow it right and, 30m beyond the turn, take the metal gate on the left, with waymarker. Stay close to the wall on your right as you descend. 150m beyond the end of the wall you come to another gate. Go through this and cut up, immediately, diagonally left, to climb for 50m rather than continuing to descend. Pause at the brow of the hill and enjoy the views into the stunning Hinchwick Valley, a little known gem of the Cotswolds. Our route follows the winding valley floor. This is a very special place and firm favourite of the authors. Drop down, steeply, beyond the gorse bushes onto level ground.

Looking down the Hinchwick Valley from Bourton Downs

Cross the horizontal telegraph poles that are part of the cross-country equestrian course and note the beech trees up to our left, which are typical of the area.

Keeping to the valley floor we are eventually re-assured by a waymarker and gate as the valley swings right. When you reach a little wooden corral on your right, a waymarker directs us diagonally right towards the buildings.

Go through the metal gate to the road. At this junction turn left towards Bourton-on-the-Hill and Broadway. Follow the road across the end of the valley and take a last look left as we reluctantly leave it. After 150m, just as the road begins to rise, leave it by the right-hand gate of the two that present themselves on your right. Go through the gate with waymarker and metal footpath sign, to enter a field. Turn sharp left and climb steeply keeping close to the fence on your left. For reference, we are running parallel to the telegraph wires that are about 50m over to the right in the field.

At the top of the hill, ignore the gate on the left, and continue beneath the telegraph wires into a corner, until just beyond the beech trees on your left, you take the stile through the wall with waymarker. Enjoy the lovely views and note the site of the ancient earthworks in the trees on the left. Turn left and follow the edge of the field with the beech trees now close on your left-hand side. Almost immediately a line of steps becomes visible on the far side of the valley ahead and this is our onward route. After 100m, leave the edge of the field at the end of the beech trees and cross diagonally left to a stile to descend into another delightful hidden valley.

At the top of the steps emerge into a field and carry on in the same direction with the wall on your left, being re-assured by a waymarker and post. There is more evidence of equestrian activity with all-weather gallops.

Straight ahead, the first glimpses of houses just above the village of Longborough come into view and, diagonally right the prominent church tower at Stow-in-the-Wold is visible. Pass a derelict barn complex on your left. Continue in the same direction to finally emerge at a lane through a pair of odd-size metal gates. ❹ Turn left and proceed 100m to the give-way sign at a junction (left Evesham and right to Stow). Cross straight over and leave the road via a path on the right into the woods to a gate with waymarker. Follow the obvious path round to the left, through the beech trees. Go through the gate onto a road and proceed straight on, down into the village of Longborough. There are delightful views of Moreton-in-Marsh ahead and slightly left, with the wooded top of Brailes Hill just above and beyond.

As you approach the village the unusual church tower comes into view on the left. As you draw level with the church, look for a left-hand turn on a path to Sezincote and Bourton-on-the-Hill. The centre of the village is just a few metres on down the road where the village green is a pleasant place to rest as is the 'Coach and Horses', a very unspoilt village pub.

However, the left-hand turn off the road gives a real sense of heading for home. Continue for 50m between hedges on an obvious track and then in the same direction with the church tower with its gargoyles on your right.

This section is well walked, generally with a wall on the right-hand side. The village of Bourton-on-the-Hill is visible straight ahead. Just beyond a small conifer plantation, keep close over to the left by the fence and cross the drive about 100m above the single dwelling to the right (do not be drawn down to it), by the cattle grid. Proceed through a kissing gate into the Sezincote estate.

A delightful piece of water becomes visible over to our right but, initially, we keep close to the wooden rail on the left for 100m and then cut down diagonally right just in front of the old fallen tree trunk (with waymarkers), just before two oaks. As we drop down towards the water the house comes into view on our left with its verdigris dome based on the Brighton Pavillion. The whole area has a delightful selection of trees especially the majestic cedars, and is pleasant at any time of the year.

Pass the water trough and aim straight across to a gate that takes you into the trees. Cross the little causeway with its two gates 20m apart. Beyond the second, bear off diagonally right as indicated by the waymarker and stay close to the rails on the right for 150m. As the rails bear round to the right, carry straight on away from them by two large trees on your left, being re-assured by the waymarker on the stump ahead.

Cross a tarmac drive and pass through two kissing gates close together and see the village of Bourton-on-the-Hill close at hand; the way is straight on and bearing slightly left, generally in line with the church tower. The approach to the village is delightful, with imposing detached residences to left and right ahead. Brailes Hill is now close by, diagonally right. Go through a gate on the edge of the village and enter a narrow lane with a tall wall on the left. Proceed for 100m, to a minor road in front of a wrought iron gate (church), and turn left uphill, passing almost immediately the restored drinking trough on your right. At the top of the rise, follow the road round to the right on join the main road through the village.

Turn left and walk past the 'Horse and Groom' pub and, at the top of the car park, cross over to the right-hand side of the road and take the bridleway (next to the 30m.p.h. sign) up a rough track. After 50m, go through the swing gate (with two metal storage silos ahead), and follow the main track sharp round to the left rather than being tempted by the little gate straight ahead.

After 75m, just before the cattle grid, turn right up a track with metal sign and waymarker. Follow this slightly sunken track with the hedge on the right as it climbs gradually. As the ground levels put at the top of the hill we are re-assured by a blue waymarker. Pause and enjoy the view back. Carry on in the same direction, this time with the woodland on your left. When you arrive at the road turn right. The outskirts of Blockley now come into view again over to our left.

A road joins from the left by a chestnut tree, but this is for reference only as we continue in the same direction, beneath the power lines. Almost immediately we are joined by woodland on our right. Care is needed to pick the left-hand turn off this road, down into the village. Just before the road swings round to the right we are joined by a taller wall on the right and it is here at the metal footpath sign that we turn left to leave the road. This is opposite a wooden door that is in the stone wall. Follow the wide track between two ivy-clad low walls. We are re-assured, after 50m, by a waymarker.

Take the right-hand of the two gates and follow the edge of the field in the same direction with large trees on your left. More of the village comes into view as we gradually lose height. Proceed through a gap in the wall to arrive at a T-junction of well-worn paths with a gate on your left. The church of Blockley comes into view for the first time. This superb setting is perhaps the finest of any of this collection of walks. Turn left through the gate.

After 200m, you arrive at a blue metal gate on your right with a stile. Take the stile and proceed straight downhill, close to the wall initially and then willows on your right. Go under the power lines as you approach Park Farm. Swing round to the left in front of the farm. Cross the stile as the pond (which is sometimes dry) comes into view and turn sharp right across the farm drive, still heading towards the church (pond on left), and go straight on down across the field, to finally emerge at the road.

Turn right and follow the road on the right-hand side, passing Rose Cottage and Lower Brook House. After a further 200m, look for a gap between the houses on the left at the back of the church and just before Colebrook House on the right. A steep tarmac drive takes you up to the right of an arched 'garage' door. By this time you may be grateful for the handrail. Pass the wrought iron gates in front of the manor house and enter the churchyard. As you walk through look out for a red granite cross, marking the grave of Captain Edward Spencer-Churchill, a cousin of Winston Churchill. Beneath the solitary light by the church door, fork right and suddenly find yourself back at the post office at the end of what we trust has been a truly memorable day. This magnificent walk stands repetition at any time of the year and, indeed, at an early start in winter on a cold bright day is as good as any in Southern England.

18

Long Compton and the Whispering Knights

> **Distance:** 11 miles/17.5 km.
> **Features:** A walk of great variety with interesting villages, remote areas, some ancient standing stones and lovely views.
> **Terrain:** Moderate/strenuous. Some climbs.
> **Maps:** Landranger 151; Pathfinder 1044.
> **Car Parking:** Roadsides near the post office.
> **Public Transport:** Stagecoach service X50 (Stratford/Oxford). Alight at Long Compton Church and walk about 100m in the Oxford direction to reach the post office.
> **Refreshments:** Pub at Whichford (half mile off route).
> **Start:** The post office on the main road at Long Compton (G.R.287327), which is on the right as you travel south through the village from the Stratford/Shipston direction. *Long Compton is an interesting village in itself with many fine buildings, notably the magnificent entrance to the churchyard.*

WITH your back to the P.O turn right and proceed to the end of the small parking area and, just before the stone monument/spring, turn right, through a gate with waymark sign. (Immediately pass the gates of Coome House as a point of reference). After 100m look for a waymark sign that takes you off the track diagonally left, (by a metal water trough), to a gate at the mid-point of the hedge in front. When you reach this point you find that you have just cut off the corner, as you rejoin the track.

The dragonfly waymarks signpost four walks, each about three miles, around the village of Long Compton, the routes when plotted on a map taking the shape of the four wings of a dragonfly. Descriptive leaflets from Stratford Tourist Information Centre.

Carry on in the same direction, with the village of Barton-on-the-Heath visible ahead. Follow the track as it curves right beyond a gate with a derelict barn just ahead. Before the track curves left, look diagonally right and spot the spire of the Church at Great Wolford. Beyond and right are the twin radio masts at Ilmington Hill. Pass beneath the telegraph wires as the farm buildings come into view. These are marked on the map but not named. ❶ Ignore the stile on the right, just before the farm buildings, and proceed straight on, leaving them on your right. Look for a gate about 100m ahead, beyond the building, and follow the path as it climbs, obviously, towards the woods.

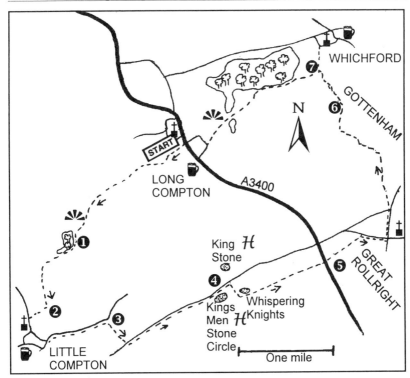

Follow the edge of the wood, looking back as the ground levels out. Our way takes us between some more farm buildings and at the junction, immediately beyond them, turn right between a barn and a single tree. Continue, sometimes muddily, along the edge of the field with the hedge on your right.

Carry on until a stone cottage is reached on the right (and sneak a view through the black wrought-iron gates in the wall). 50m beyond the cottage is a large, single prefabricated barn on the left (with diesel tank). Turn left before it (between barn and hedge), and descend towards Little Compton with the hedge on the left.

Horton Farm quickly comes into view **❷**, but before entering the front garden, take the sign through a gap on the left and carry on down the field with the hedge on your right. At the corner go back through a gap; don't rejoin the farm drive, but turn left and then immediately right and follow the hedge to a small wooden footbridge in the corner. Beyond it turn immediately left and follow the edge of the field with the hedge on the left. At the bottom of the field is a stream. Turn right and follow the line of the stream through a gate to join the road by the '30' signs.

Turn left (passing the cemetery on your right). Continue along the lane to a T-junction where you turn right with Old Post Office Row on your right. As you see the signs for Reed College ahead, bear round to the left into Church Lane and follow it to the end. At this junction (there is a children's play area on the left) our route is left (G.R.262302), but you should take two minutes to follow the pavement right for 50m to the twin pillars (with globes) which is the entrance to Reed College.

Anyway, back at the junction, having turned left, pass Hope Cottage and two black barns on the left and follow the road as it curves right to eventually leave the village along Oakham Road with a line of six garages on your left. As you climb the straight road out of the village, glance left and spot the line of our descent earlier, on the opposite side of the little valley. Go past the entrance to Langstone Farm on the right (with twin grain hoppers) and continue with the uphill slog, which is well worth it – honestly!

At the top of the climb, as the road swings round to the left, turn right through a gate (with waymark). ❸ A bridleway follows the wall on the right but our route curves round to the left along the Macmillan Way which we follow for a little way. Keep to the edge of the field, with a tall hedge on your left, and pause to enjoy the view as a reward for the road climb. At the gap, carry straight on as the white cottages come into view ahead and slightly right. Join the road at a white gate (and metal footpath sign). Turn left.

The level road walking gives time to look at the view with the village of Chipping Norton over to the right. Ignore the left-hand turn back to Little Compton and carry straight on to the Rollright Stones.

Pass the house named Saffron Heights, go over the crossroads and look for a gap on the left to spot our starting point at Long Compton. However, don't leave the road. Continue on for about a quarter of a mile to reach the King's Men (small admission charge), a Bronze Age unditched stone circle, dating back to about 1500BC, and thought to have been used for ritual purposes. On the left is the solitary King Stone, reached via a stile. Legend has it that a king who set out to conquer England was turned to stone by a witch. ❹

About 200m beyond this stile (about 100m beyond the sign for Wyatts Tea-room) look for a right-hand turn to leave the road by a green gate beside a 'No pavement for 200 yards' sign, with a tall hedge on your left. You shortly reach the Whispering Knights, the remains of a long barrow burial mound. It is said that when children count the number of stones in the circle they find a different number each time! The Whispering Knights are said to have suffered the same fate as their king.

Past the Whispering Knights carry straight on for 100m and, at the trees in front of you, turn left and take the stile. Go straight across the field to another stile. Cross the farm track and carry straight on, this time with the hedge on the left, then in a second field with a hedge on the right.. Leave the field on the far side, at the trees, and cut down diagonally left, as indicated, to the road. ❺

The Whispering Knights

Turn right on the main road for 20m and then cross over and ascend the steps opposite (not immediately obvious). Carry on in the same direction, at right angles to the road, across the field (with initially some trees immediately on your left). Go through a hedge gap and continue in a second field with a hedge on your left. The village of Great Rollright eventually begins to appear and after going through a narrow wooded area you emerge at the road at double wooden gates, and turn right.

The former village pub at Great Rollright is now a private dwelling – a calamitous fact that we discovered when using an old O.S. map.

Just beyond the village sign for Great Rollright you arrive at a crossroads. Turn left here towards Whichford and Banbury and follow the road, with trees on your left, to the first junction on the left (about 100m after the end of the trees). Leave the road at this junction via the gate straight ahead where there is a metal footpath sign next to a Give Way sign.

Go diagonally across the corner of the field for 100m to the waymark post and stile. Carry straight on across the next field, looking for a waymarked stile, in the general direction of the low farm buildings. Go diagonally across the farm drive to immediately enter another field via the waymarkers. After 100m (in the same direction) pause on the far side of the field. We are quite close to the farm buildings on our left. The path goes straight on across the field but in the event of crop obstruction you may be forced to keep to the left, nearer the farm buildings, and to follow the edge of the field for about 150m to the far side and a wire fence.

The land falls away quite sharply here into a delightful valley, with Long Compton visible down to the left. Turn right and follow the edge of the field to a corner where there is a stile and waymarker. Beyond the stile turn sharp left, downhill, with water troughs on your left, to a small wooden gate. Beyond this our way is less distinct as we enter a large prairie-like field.

Pause for a moment and look up to the ridge beyond (and slightly right) to spot a large barn among some pine trees (Doctor's Barn on the O.S. map) which is on our onward route.

Continue straight downhill into a little bowl with the hedge over to the left (we lose sight of the barn). At the bottom of the slope there is a single stand-alone oak tree on the left for reference. About 200m beyond the tree the hedge swings left to the corner and we begin to swing sharp right and contour round the hill without losing any more height. There is no defined path so don't be drawn down to the left corner of the field.. Another hedge is now about 100m over to the left and the chimney and roof of Gottenham **6** comes into view. We aim for the left-hand end of the wooden fence that surrounds the property.

On reaching the fence ignore the gap in the hedge that is 30m over to the left, but rather follow the line of the hedge for a further 100m to pick up a waymark post and waymarker on he same side.

Descend the steep steps to a stile and cross the stream. Turn right and, after 30m, go through a gap and proceed uphill close to the line of the hedge on your left. Just beyond where the ground levels out and the trees and hedge on your left finish, you arrive at a farm track. **7** Turn left on the track as indicated and look ahead to see Doctor's Barn over to the right (this is a large Dutch barn and farm complex). As you draw level with the barn enjoy some spectacular views over to your right and pick out the windmill on the escarpment above the villages at Brailes in the middle distance.

Carry straight on along the obvious track in the same direction, now joined by a tall hedge on your left. Just before you reach Whichford Woods look over to the right and pick out the top of the church tower at Whichford (the rest of the village remains hidden beyond the convex slope). Carry straight on as the route joins the edge of the woods on your right and our outward journey from Great Rollright is visible over to the left. Continue straight on at a waymark post and proceed for another 400m to another post with a huge collection of waymarkers! Leave the edge of the woods here and proceed diagonally left across the field. Proceed to the trees and waymarker on the far side (this is normally an obvious path). Approaching the trees cross straight over a track that divides the rest of the field.

At the trees our destination is visible once again in a delightful position. Descend the wide track through the trees to a stile and skirt the gorse bushes following the line of two waymark posts. Just beyond the second post (where there is a concrete drinking trough) cut downhill, slightly right, to a gate and stile.

Beyond the stile keep over left towards the hedge to another stile (hidden), and so reach a track. Cross this and go diagonally right (waymarker) towards the village. Cross a footbridge and continue forward to reach Vicarage Road. Turn right along this to the main road where a right turn will return you to your starting point at the post office.

Before you leave, the church is well worth a visit. You enter the churchyard by an impressive lych gate that was rebuilt in the 1960s. Parts of the church are Norman and the ancient doors are dated 1620. There is much of interest inside the church, described in a very informative leaflet that is available inside the church.

The church and Gate House at Long Compton

Index

100

Looking towards Bannam's Wood from an anciemt track above the B4480
(Walk 1)

Also from Meridian...

COUNTRY WALKS IN WARWICKSHIRE AND WORCESTERSHIRE
by Des Wright

Twenty circular walks that explore some of the two counties most attractive areas. The walking is easy, mostly on the flat and with few climbs. Distances range from 2½ to 8½ miles although some can be combined to give longer walks.

ISBN 1 869922 33 6. £5.95. 96 pages. 16 photographs. 21 maps.

MORE COUNTRY WALKS IN WARWICKSHIRE AND WORCESTERSHIRE
by Des Wright

A second collection of circular walks in two fine counties from a popular author. As in his first collection the walking is not difficult with few climbs. Distances range from 4½ to 11½ miles, with most walks having a shorter option of between 1½ and 8 miles.

ISBN 1 869922 37 9. £5.95. 112 pages. 22 photographs. 20 maps.

WALKS IN WARWICKSHIRE AND WORCESTERSHIRE
A Third Collection
by Des Wright

This third collection of walks by a popular author explores further some of the attractive countryside in two West Midlands counties. Distances range between 2 and 9.5 miles, with one rather more strenuous walk of 14 miles

ISBN 1-869922-44-1. Price £6.95.112 pages. 24 illustrations. 22 maps.

WALKS TO WET YOUR WHISTLE
by Roger Seedhouse

Eighteen walks covering some of the most beautiful countryside in Shropshire and along its Staffordshire borders, each providing an opportunity to visit a pub in which the walker will feel welcome. Distances range between 7 and 11½ miles but each has a shorter alternative of between 2¾ and 5¼ miles.

ISBN 1 869922 34 4. £6.95. 112 pages. 17 photographs. 18 maps.

MORE WALKS TO WET YOUR WHISTLE
by Roger Seedhouse.

Following the continuing success of his first book Roger Seedhouse has prepared a second collection of walks with a pub, each having shorter and longer alternatives

ISBN 1 869922 36 0. £6.95. 112 pages. 24 photographs. 18 maps.

WALKS AROUND THE MALVERNS
by Roy Woodcock

The Malvern Hills and their surroundings provide magnificent opportunities for rambling and the twenty walks in this book cover the entire range of hills together with some of the delightful countryside nearby. Distances range from 2 to 8 miles, plus a leg stretcher of between 10 and 16 miles (depending on the starting point) that takes in the full length of the ridge.

ISBN 1 869922 32 8. £5.95. 112 pages. 32 illustrations. 20 maps.

Meridian Books
40 Hadzor Road • Oldbury • West Midlands • B68 9LA
Prices correct January 2003
Please write for our complete catalogue